The Adventures of the Audrey Eleanor

ALSO AVAILABLE BY DAWN KOSTELNIK:

The White Girl (2014)

Current publications can be seen in:
The Northern Journal
The Yukon Times
The Whitehorse Star

The Adventures of the

AUDREY ELEANOR

The Adventures of the Audrey Eleanor

DAWN KOSTELNIK has 76 titles published on kobo.com and amazon.com.

The author is currently working on a new novel, WOMAN WALKING. This will be a fictionalized story based on fact. As a little girl of four winters, Mary, a First Nations Child, walks through Mother Summer and almost into Father Winter from her far away birthplace in the Yukon Territory. Her parents now choose to live on the shores of one of Canada's grandest lakes, The Great Bear. Many winters later, her life trail is coming to an end. She has visions of her pathway to the stars, footsteps leading her to dance around the fire of the Borealis with her ancestors. Her eyes are old and weary from many trials, she stands with bowed head in Hiroshima Japan in 1998, the 50th Anniversary of the drop of the atomic bomb. She ponders her participation in this devastation. How will she face the old ones?

Typesetting: Massive Graphic, in Minion 10pt on 14
Cover design and layout: Massive Graphic (massivegraphic.ca)
ISBN 978-1-511717-30-4

*This book is dedicated to my son Bob and
my daughter Kaitlin!*

————⌐∘∕∘∕∘⌐————

With sincerest gratitude to Jim Butler, Editor of the *Whitehorse Star*, for taking a chance and letting me keep my "voice" in both The White Girl Series and the Adventures of the Audrey Eleanor. It is people in positions of power, like Jim Butler, who have the strength to take on a new artist and not edit them into obscurity. Unfortunately, it seems that the safe path is much easier to follow and we are forced to write based on auto-correct for acceptance and the world has become homogenous. There are few people with Mr. Butler's self-assurance and strength, and I have been fortunate. Thank you, Jim.

PREFACE

These stories as presented in separate chapters previously made individual appearances in the Whitehorse Star Newspaper in Whitehorse, Yukon Territory, Canada. The Whitehorse Star has served the Yukon and Alaska since its conception in 1900. In October 2013, re-runs of the **WHITE GIRL** began to make weekly appearances in **THE NORTHERN JOURNAL** (norj.ca). On January 2, 2014, **ADVENTURES OF THE AUDREY ELEANOR** motored into the pages of the fledgling newspaper, The Yukon Times (yukontimes.com).

In June of 2008, the first of many, **ADVENTURES OF THE AUDREY ELEANOR** appeared in print in the Whitehorse Star. This one-time adventure series turned into a bi-monthly, full-page column that ran until its conclusion in December 2010. Cameo appearances popped up until May 2013, with fans demanding, "just one more Adventure, please". There are a few more in the queue that will be cast out to sea at a future date.

The birth of the **WHITE GIRL** was on January 7, 2011 in the Whitehorse Star. The White Girl is True North Stories about growing up in the Arctic. These stories appeared as full-page, bi-monthly columns as well. As individual units they are being published in a different format in the Northern Journal in Fort Smith, NWT.

I hope that the Adventures of the Audrey Eleanor inspire others to follow their dreams of casting off the lines of responsibility and embracing each day as it comes. If the Captain and I can do it, anyone can follow suit and will most likely do as well or better than we did. It was one of the best times of my life, regardless of the winter of storms and yes, even the rats.

Become the captain of your fate, the master of your destiny. Start your journey by reading the Adventures of the Audrey Eleanor, and may your life never be the same.

To My Captain,

where you lead, I will follow...not

always willingly, but without you, my love,

there is no adventure.

TABLE OF CONTENTS

North To Alaska

FROM PRINCE RUPERT, BC
TO SKAGWAY ALASKA

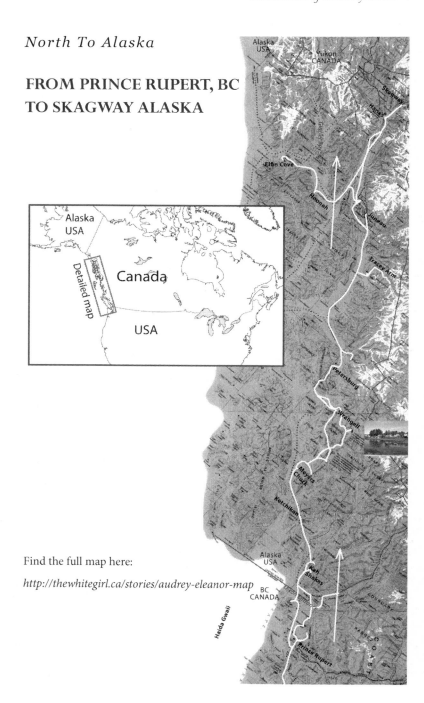

Find the full map here:

http://thewhitegirl.ca/stories/audrey-eleanor-map

Yukoners fell in love with a 54', 1948 wooden yacht. From June of 2008 until December 2010, a worldwide following read about the adventures of the Audrey Eleanor in the Whitehorse Star. We are proud to bring these adventures to you once again.

North To Alaska

THE ADVENTURES OF THE AUDREY ELEANOR

TAKING ON THE BIG BOYS

The Captain, Rick Cousins, spent the winter retrofitting Audrey in McLean's Shipyard in Prince Rupert, B.C. McLean's Shipyard is reputed to be one of the oldest working shipyards on the west coast of Canada. This a great place to be when you have an old boat. I had to return to Whitehorse, as our home there had been flooded. The three week restoration work on the house turned into a four and a half month project that was beyond belief. I don't wish an insurance claim on anyone.

By the time the Alaska State Ferry dropped me off in the terminal at Prince Rupert, the Captain had made the most of his winter. With the help of our friend, Bruce Cairns, he removed old rusted fuel tanks from the hold and built new tanks to replace them. This is not an easy thing. You have to remove these tanks through the back wall of the stateroom, so the aft deck had to be modified. Rick decided to install sewage holding tanks in the back head (toilet). The foc'sle already had one. Our plan was to visit marine parks and areas with low flushing bays, and you should take your poop with you when you go!

In January, days before I was forced to return to Whitehorse, the temperature dropped to minus 12° Celsius in Seal Cove, Prince Rupert. Minus 12 on the black ocean is bone chilling cold. Salt water does freeze and so does toothpaste. Walking on the docks and gunnels is dangerous, and falling into a bay of liquid ice will end your life. There are few people crazy enough to be out on the docks; McLean's Shipyard has shut down their operation until the weather warms up. There is no one out here to rescue a sinker in the sea; it would be difficult to drag yourself out, clawing over iced boards.

The cold makes getting into bed a serious challenge; who can sit up the longest so as not to have to be the first one to crawl between the icy sheets? We have since learned that if power is available, an electric blanket is your best friend…it gets rid of the damp, as well as the cold.

It is now finally springtime! The Audrey Eleanor is registered in Haines, Alaska; all that is left to do is paint her serial numbers on her bow and her name and port of registration on her stern.

It's time to cast off. Prince Rupert has been Audrey's home for the past twelve years. We purchased her in the summer of 2003, and are finally taking her to her new home in Haines, Alaska. We want her as close to Whitehorse as possible. As the raven flies, this will be six hundred kilometres north through the famous Inside Passage. It will be our maiden voyage, but most certainly not Audrey's.

Both Rick and I have extensive and varied fresh water and wilderness skills. Rick has flown bush planes, retrieved planes from lakes, built boats, and welded underwater from the Arctic to the Antarctic. I grew up on the Mackenzie River and on the coast of the Arctic Ocean. Armed with a powerful dream, the Canadian Power Squadron Navigation course and more enthusiasm than experience, we are headed "NORTH TO ALASKA." Yeah, Johnny Horton!!

Rick has concentrated his energy on ensuring that his Perkins engines purr. We have heard horror stories of crossing the infamous Dixon Entrance. Rick wants no hesitation in the engines in the event of a rough crossing; the man is a psychic. We are ready, the seas are calm, a few wisps of fog give depth to the majestic mountains. It's six a.m. and we are underway. We are heading home, north to Alaska. Go north, the rush is on!

This is wonderful! Audrey's stately bow slices through the sea. We traverse the shipyard maze and are cruising past the floating Esso fuel docks. Not too bad. We begin to feel cocky enough to consider docking at Cow Bay and running up for a coffee to go. Docking a yacht of this size (she weighs 30 tonnes), especially without a bow thruster is intimidating the first hundred times you try it. The Prince Rupert Yacht Club is straight ahead. There are two multi-million dollar U.S. yachts tied to the north end of the dock, leaving plenty of room for us to bring our bow in.

The Captain steers Audrey's bow straight on to the dock with the intent of gently swinging and bringing her stern alongside. Suddenly the current grabs a handful of Audrey's 30 tonnes, and we have no control. We speed up and are on a bow-on-beam collision course with those shiny metal mini-ships. The huge steel bows of these metal demons look determined to thrust themselves through Audrey's oak ribs and pierce her Perkins hearts. The thought of a probable lawsuit brought on by the south of the border boys pierces my own heart.

I throw out our now ridiculously-small bumpers and prepare for impact. The big boys we are about to impale ourselves on are confident enough in their bulk that they have no defense bumpers dangling off their sides. What's a girl to do? Throw herself in front of her yacht, of course.

I have no idea what is going through my mind. I am five feet tall with a medium build, but I must be super woman! I position myself between them and us. I WILL BE THE BUMPER! I do manage to slow us down enough so that when impact occurs it isn't significant enough to even wake the sleeping crew. At least, the lights don't come on. Now what? I am wedged between grinding metal and petrified wood ships!

How does it feel to be the human filling in this sandwich, you ask? I realize how deadly the situation is when I look up to see that the Captain's face is deathly white, I am having difficulty breathing. Rick is slamming levers and manipulating the throttles trying to get us off of these guys. Audrey's thirty tonnes are slowing grinding down the steel sides of the yachts with me acting as the resistance between them and us; this is not fun anymore.

The Goddess returns and the tide turns, stops, or whatever it does. Maybe the Captain figured things out and like nothing had ever happened, we gently swing back out the way we came in. I can breath, the yachts sleep on and we don't have to sell all of our future grandchildren to satisfy a possible lawsuit.

"God hates a coward." We will try this docking thing again. Besides, now we really want that coffee. We have a new approach and Audrey gently swings into place beside the big boys on the dock as if to say, "Hey boys, that's all you get."

We wobble up the ramp to Cowpuccinos in Cow Bay, looking for coffee; tequila would have been better. So what will Dixon Entrance bring?

...if only we knew then what we know now. That will be another one of the Adventures of the Audrey Eleanor.

North To Alaska

DIXON ENTRANCE

We are onboard the **Audrey Eleanor,** a custom-built fifty four foot 1948 wooden yacht headed north to Alaska. After a near disaster with two multi-million dollar U.S. yachts at the Prince Rupert Yacht Club in Prince Rupert, B.C., we are ready to take on Dixon Entrance. This is our first salt water crewing experience.

Relief at feeling solid ground under our feet at Kah Shakes Cove, our first stop in Alaska after broaching the Audrey Eleanor in huge seas crossing the infamous Dixon Entrance. The Captain holds firm the Terra Firma.

The shortest route out of Prince Rupert is north through Metlakatla Passage. We decide that we are not ready to take on the narrow, twisting Metalka, with its range markers and rocks, and opt instead for the route that allows the B.C. and Alaska State Ferries safe access out of the harbour.

We cruise serenely by the docked Alaska State ferry with sleepy passengers waving from the decks. Audrey's unique design attracts attention wherever she goes; she is a show-off. We slip past the ferry and run smack into a wall of fog.

You literally hit fog walls, banks, whatever you prefer to call them. We slide through the curtain and are in a muffled world of soft greys and cool whites. Nothing appears to be real as the fog climbs up on the bow and pulls its wall of white down behind it. Everything disappears. In this muffled cocoon, sounds are distorted; it is surreal and very dangerous. Wooden ships or boats often don't show up on radar; we are a ghost ship moving undetected through a shipping lane.

We do have radar on board our ship. We had both assumed the other knew how to work it. Neither of us knows how to make this ancient gadget work, but the Captain is a better bet; he has used instruments such as this when flying airplanes. I head for the bow to stand watch or, more accurately, to listen for approaching objects. What would a floating dead-head sound like?

The Captain calls me back into the saloon. He's worried that if we hit something, or something hits us, the impact will drop me into the salt chuck. Thanks to his bush pilot experience, he's figured out the radar. Now we'll be able to see our demise before it hits us.

A few feet further, and the fog drops away as quickly as it came; we head face-first into the sunshine. This is the point in the channel where we take a starboard turn and are now in Hecate Straight. The seas begin to build. Audrey's displacement hull easily cuts through the chop that is bouncing other boats in the area around. I wonder how well I will handle it if it gets really bouncy...how well will Audrey handle it? We haven't had her out of Prince Rupert harbour and aren't sure what she's made of. Beautiful little islands slip by and the people on the lighthouse wave enthusiastically as we cruise northward.

Dundas Island appears to our portside. (Am I starting to sound like I know something?) We navigate toward the island and our anchorage at Brundigee Bay. One of the great things about traveling at this time of year is that there are virtually no other boats on the water and, consequently, no audiences.

You can drop and drag your anchor to your heart's content, or until hand cranking 100 feet of chain and one hundred and fifty feet of rode wears you out. My arms are still sore from doing battle with the U.S. yachts in Prince Rupert. This has to be done right if we are to get any sleep tonight...and I did mention...this is the first time we have anchored the Audrey Eleanor.

Huge orange lion's mane jellyfish attach themselves to our rode. Resembling alien "blobs" from a bad sci-fi movie, I believe that during the night they plan to slither up the rode, shanghai our ship and drop our bodies in the darkness of the bay. We sleep through the night; I do not believe that if we had drug the anchor or been eaten by lion's mane jellyfish I would have noticed.

We plan to get through Dixon Entrance as early as possible. Winds tend to raise in the afternoon, so the earlier the start, the better. I look overboard to see how far the orange aliens have made it up the rode, and, oh my, are those diesel fuel rainbows that I see on the water?' One of the fuel filters has blown a seal. An early start is no longer reality. Rick disappears into the "Troll Hole", otherwise known as the engine compartment, to deal with the busted seal.

The decision is to make breakfast and enjoy the scenery. We are really doing this! Casting free from land, assuming total responsibility for ourselves and our boat, heading NORTH TO ALASKA! We had gotten to the point of both buying a boat and learning about a life on the high seas, or of simply shutting up and staying to run the rivers of the Yukon. JUST DO IT - We just did it, finally!

At noon, we are ready to cross the infamous Dixon Entrance. We are half an hour out of Brundigee Bay; there are bright blue skies with a light breeze tweaking the water's surface, but no Dixon demons here. What we don't realize is that we have started out at a full slack tide; as the tide turns, the winds tend to pick up.

The winds are now howling down all three of the enormous channels, and we are headed out into open ocean in the direction of the Queen Charlotte Islands. The tides are running hard against us and the wind is blowing the tops off the waves. A huge volume of water is dumping in a massive deluge, pouring down on us from Alaska, British Columbia and, I am sure, Japan. We will sink, we will be drowned.

The wind is blowing hard against the waves. We have confused seas, the waves are having a nervous breakdown, pounding water is bouncing and slamming us everywhere.

The Captain has thrown his chair out of the way and he is working the helm with his whole body, feet braced wide apart for stability. I run through the boat, duct-taping the slamming doors shut, trying to stop the cupboards from spewing their contents all over the floors. The noise of banging and crashing is deafening. It's too rough to stand; I have to crawl back to the main saloon.

I see the Captain working the helm, battling to take control of his ship. The waves throw us sideways; he hangs on and with all of his might fights the wheel to take us in the opposite direction. There is nothing that I can do except to try to hold on. I open the starboard door in the main saloon and have a death clench on the doorframe. The opening is about three feet by three feet and my thoughts at this moment are, "If this ships going down, I am not going to be trapped inside. I will not go down with this ship!"

We are falling; Audrey hits the bottom in the trough of the wave, full-on her precarious beam. She shudders; the impact reverberates through her hull and feels like she is breaking apart at the seams. I have braced myself in the doorway to prepare for the impact; I am slammed against the doorframe. It takes everything I have to keep from being hurtled into the boiling black sea.

I cannot believe it! She is coming back around. I'm swung hard back against the chart table. The Captain is fighting for our lives. We begin to fall again, this time we don't fall as far and we hit part way down on her side, the best of the worst, and backward we roll.

The Captain has control. I can feel the change in Audrey. He's in charge of our ship and he's going to take us out. He looks at me and I yell at him, "Just drive this *@#! boat; don't you dare look at me!"

He can't be distracted if he's going to get us out. He said later that he was sure that I was having a heart attack. The waves are huge… my eyes are huger. The waves are bigger than Audrey and oh no…He's heading further out to sea! I am going to have a heart attack! I am pleading, "Please, please, don't go out there!"

We have to head further out to sea in order to tack back. We are in 18 foot seas and have no experience on turning a 54 foot ship around in this life-swallowing maw of an ocean.

"OH MY!" The Captain is now using Audrey as a giant surfboard and we are surfing the huge waves. We are going to make it!

Our friend Don Pilsworth insisted that we take his survival suits. We have them, they are on board...in the back closet. In a very short time, we went from a light breeze on sparkling blue waters, to fighting for our lives. We could not physically get to those suits, never mind put them on. It was simply too late.

Foggy Bay is considered the first good anchorage after the Dixon Entrance. One look at the waves breaking in the entrance to Foggy Bay and we keep going. We anchor at Kah Shakes Cove and when we finally shut down the engines... I start to cry.

P.S. This is a popular story with the gang at the Gold Rush Inn in Whitehorse. Hello to all of you, save us a beer.

North To Alaska

THE GIRLS ON THE DOCKS

My daughter-in-law, Shellane, on the bow of the Audrey Eleanor *in the Lynn Canal between Skagway and Haines, Alaska.*

There are few women who live on the docks. When I happen to meet these women, there an instant kindred connection. Our conversations are about boating, but with a feminine twist. One of my many rants to my kids is, the more you know, the less you will learn. It is great to listen to the experiences of these ladies. The information they pass on is exceptional and has contributed in unusual ways to my life to this day.

The curiosity of it is that the three women whom I recall most clearly were named Jenny. These were my first teachers. Jenny off of the Jenny B in Ketchikan, Alaska, was the floating dentist's wife. Jenny from Smithers, B.C., she and her husband were retrofitting the Debby J in McLean's

Shipyard, and little Jenny, the dock handywoman who went places that most men can't.

Jenny from the Jenny B is an enigma and would be anywhere that she went. She and her husband built the boat, Jenny B, from the hull up. The boat progressed in stages and as her children grew, so did the boat. They raised two daughters aboard; the girls finally went aground when they needed to attend university. Their mother home schooled them while they floated through Alaska for all of their childhood years.

As the dentist's wife, she was also his receptionist. She met clients at the stern and escorted them into the dentist's chair, then helped them off the boat with a smile and a Kleenex. We arrive onboard for tea; she appears in the saloon with her usual perfectly coiffed hair, a blouse and skirt with one of those little frilly aprons that matches her shoes and nails. It is amazing.

I am ecstatic if I manage to haul the laundry topside and have clean socks. How does this woman do this? In addition to maintaining this immaculate, if unusual, appearance, she cleaned and sanitized all of the dentistry equipment and had dinner on the table by six. In her world, this was how it was done.

She was by no means a plastic lady. This is her style and by the Goddess she can take charge of the helm, read the charts, tie her boat up or drop the anchor whenever needed. Men rule the sea, she contributed to the feminine. She is truly a good person and a very nice lady. The fishermen went out of their way to be courteous to her; she added a wonderful softness where there is little of it.

The Jenny off of the Debbie J is a formidable lady. The first sailboat that she and her husband bought was a 35 foot something, she wasn't sure what. They took a crash course in sailing one weekend in Vancouver and then set out onto the briny sea. She said that it took several weeks for her to relax and realize that the great walls of seawater weren't going to crash down and swamp them from behind. They were out in the blue water and onto 35 foot swells.

They went from the 35 foot mystery boat to a 65 foot Robertson steel sailboat. Their kids were growing and by now they had sailed south to Mexico and through the Panama Canal. They had been at sea for a year, it was expansion time. This type of expansion is not to be confused with one "footitis", which is common in boating circles. The "footitis" virus (I think the strain originates in Texas) attacks people who think that they need one more foot of boat for whatever reason. Commonly the reason is either to haul more "stuff" or to keep up with the Davy Joneses.

We have a rule on board Audrey, that we now carry over into our shore lives. If you bring something aboard, you have to take something off. This makes you pay attention to what essential truly means. Does it nourish you? Keep you warm and dry, or provide you with healthy diversion? (Books and music are essential by the way.) How much do you really need? Stuff weighs you down, it anchors you on the hard and it sinks you at sea.

Back to the 65 foot Robertson, they had engine problems outside of New York harbour and were going to have to come in under full sail. Coming into any harbour with a large boat is hard on the nerves, an unknown harbour is extremely painful, and a New York type harbour on any day of the year is my nightmare.

Jenny said that they had to choose between their love of living at sea and paying to insure their sailboat; they chose their love. They did not insure the sailboat, and they were prepared to step off of the boat and hand over their keys if they encountered a problem. Into the harbour under full sail they come! Kids are in their positions with mom and dad at the helm, praying hard.

People are scrambling over each other trying to get their precious boats out of the way of this larger-than-should-be-free-sailing boat. It is really exciting! Dad swings her hard to portside, there is only one space big enough to tie up. The kids drop the sails and they gently swing into the berth. Jenny said she stepped off holding the ropes, shaking in her boots, hoping that she would not throw up and praying that it didn't show. A large crowd had gathered, and with shaking hands Jenny calmly tied her up and said to the kids, "OK, let's do lunch."

This Jenny explained to me that you never eat crab on your boat. Crab is served dockside on some kind of makeshift table with lots of good friends, wine and butter. You simply cannot get all of the small crab parts picked up and this attracts nasty critters that will cause grief in the long run. I know from personal experience that at sunrise the damned birds love to run around the top deck pecking at the crab pieces that I've missed. This dance floor is right above our stateroom; there is no sleep with the funky seagull going on above your head.

Little Jenny is less than five feet in height and weighs possibly 80 pounds. I would guess her age at somewhere between thirty and eighty. Some days she looked thirty, and some days she looked eighty. If you were looking for a hard worker for cheap, you called Jenny.

Because of her size, she could fit down into the stinky bilges and fish holds that most adult-sized people couldn't and wouldn't get into. Her boyfriend was the shiftless kind, didn't work unless Jenny absolutely couldn't. He was known as "Rusty" on the docks. Whenever someone approached him to do a job of any kind, his response was always, "Well I'm a little rusty at that." Hence, he was known as Rusty to all.

Jenny would spend the whole day down in a tight, smelly, dark old hold working with nasty chemicals and come bouncing out at the end of the day with a big smile on her face. She was a voracious gardener. Her little trailer was an oasis in an otherwise tin can wasteland. When we left McLean's Shipyard in Prince Rupert, she gave me a clump of for-get-me-nots that I transplanted into my son Bob's yard here in White-horse. Forgot to tell you about that Bobby. I believe that they are still there.

May was an exceptionally hot month in Prince Rupert. Jenny had been mucking out the hold of a large tugboat that originally had been scheduled to be scuttled. A new owner had stepped in just before the final countdown. This big tug was a mess. Jenny was determined to make this tugboat shine. I don't know what she was using for cleaning agents, or for paints either, but she had spent the whole morning and part of the scorching afternoon swimming in toxic brine.

At two o'clock in the middle of this heated afternoon, she came wandering down the dock not her usual perky self.

"Are you alright, Jenny?"

"Yes," came the reply. "But I think I'm dehydrated."

The water had been shut off on the docks, and of course we had chosen this day to clean our water tanks.

"How does a beer sound?"

The big smile was back.

"That would be absolutely wonderful," she said.

She perched on the sawhorse with her beer, took a big swig and fell over backwards, unconscious.

By the time that I got off the boat and on to the dock, her eyes were wide open and she was staring in wonder at the sky.

"Wow, what was in that beer?" was all that she said. We drove her home.

P.S. The Debby J was being retrofitted from a fish boat into a global gypsy. The 30 foot troller had a gardener engine in her that topped out at 8 knots but only burned 3 gals of fuel per hour. The Debby J and crew were headed for South America, Chile in particular. They are probably out there still, we wish them well.

North To Alaska

DOCKSIDE IN KETCHIKAN, ALASKA

I love tying up at the docks. Anchoring out is wonderful, but being able to meet new and unusual people is always welcome after weeks of challenges and solitude. One of my favourite marinas is Thomas Basin in Ketchikan, Alaska. It has an entry that is easy to miss, as it is tucked in behind a great sea wall and the cruise ship dock. This solid wall of cruise ships makes Skagway look like a sleepy fishing port in comparison…the crowds and noise are exciting for a few days, but only just a few. Soon, you begin to listen for the bell that herds the cattle back on board the cruise ship and THEN you head for town. At night time, a forty foot high wall of ship lights flickers shadowy daylight to the docks.

On our first moorage in Ketchikan we are fortunate to borrow a tem-

A combination of cruise ships and live-aboards creates an interesting environment in Thomas Basin, a marina in Ketchikan, Alaska.

porary berth from a fisherman who is out trying his luck with his fishing nets. The Harbour Master shows up minutes after we've docked, gives his nod of approval and welcomes us to Ketchikan. This is our first port of entry into the U.S. after heading north from Prince Rupert, B.C., Canada.

The Captain calls customs and asks how they would like us to proceed…the customs lady is very nice, she also welcomes us and states that she is glad that we have made port. They had been expecting us two days earlier and were concerned. We had reported to customs in Prince Rupert and given them a rough ETA for Ketchikan. The infamous Dixon Entrance gave us a run for our money and our lives, so we were a little late.

It is suggested that we walk up to the pink building that houses customs and sign in. We can see it from the stern. The Potlatch Bar is at the top of the ramp; it has a laundry attached to the side of it and is definitely the centre of all social activity on the docks. If you want to check the weather, the fishing conditions, or find someone who knows how to deal with a 32 consta-volt system off of an antique boat, this is the place.

The top of the ramp features an assortment of bicycles, all coloured rust in different degrees. These bikes are a definite sign of "live-aboards" on the docks, a dirty word in some places of imagined importance. Live-aboards are people who live aboard their boats, seafaring gypsies they are. Sadly, some of them end up as Harbour Queens (boats that for one reason or another never leave the docks). I would like to say in defence of that, I believe anyway of living on the ocean is better than no way of living on the ocean.

Live-aboards are some of the most interesting people that you'll ever meet. There are plenty of questions about boats and living aboard that are never-ending to a greenhorn. These are the people that may answer your questions. They need to be approached cautiously, never presume that they want talk to you, never mind that they want to answer your obviously childish questions. After direct attempts at establishing contact, I've learned that reverse physiology seems to be the best non-approach. Swabbing the decks is always open to comment and the makings of new friends.

Audrey's good looks and age attract the boating community and soon repair stories and preventative ideas spring upward and the conversation begins to grow skyward. There always needs to be an inspection of each others' boats, and this should now be discussed over coffee on board, of course. It's so much fun!!

A 32 volt system always opens dialogue…things like, "Oh, yeah, I remember that, my grandpa had that on his fishing boat," from a fifty year old. When looking for parts for this antiquated system that we use aboard the *Audrey Eleanor,* they are difficult to find, but the quest may lead you to people like Only.

His name is Only; he is a draft dodger that lives on an island close to Ketchikan that is populated with other draft dodgers from the 60's. They have since received amnesty, but their ideals and lifestyle have developed into a self-sufficient, "there is nothing wrong with things as they are." They challenge any form of authority kind of idealism that we used to see in the Yukon. It kind of felt like the good old days in Dawson City. They believe in barter and bow before the god of "hoardism". (Throw nothing away, ever.)

Thank goodness they throw nothing away, they have 32-volt system parts for all kinds of things. Only is our man. He replaces our consta-volt and we have to repay him with rum in the Potlatch Bar.

Only also shows up to work bringing us dinner, fresh red snapper filets that one of the fisherman is giving away on the dock to locals. The fishermen setting deep nets for halibut are also pulling up red snappers, by regulation they are required to "process" them. It isn't unusual to see huge red snappers floating around the dock with teaspoon-sized filets scooped out of their sides. This minimum of work in "processing" deems that the silly regulation requirement has been met.

The floating dentist and his wife, Jennifer, pulled into the berth across from us on our last night at Thomas Basin. Their boat is homemade, called the "Jenny", and is about 45 feet in length; she is a big-bottomed girl, with a great wide beam of 15 feet.

Wide beams are lovely things in rough seas and I have a definite soft spot for the ride and security of them. The Jenny and her crew have been cruising the coast of Alaska for 25 years. They now winter in the Southern U.S., but spent numerous years living aboard in Alaska. They raised their two daughters aboard, but moved south when the girls needed higher education.

Appointments are set up in the early spring for all small coastal communities, and the "Jenny" then spends the summer stopping at all the ports and fixing teeth. You enter the boat from a walk-through on the aft deck; plants and two small trees are growing in pots that frame the doorway. The first room you enter is the dental office, complete with all of the dental equipment that you never want to see.

There is a full-sized dental chair that can be curtained off from the reception area; it is exactly what you would see in a dental office located ashore, with a little wave motion thrown in. Those of you who come into marinas under power, thinking that the "no wake" signs are meant for somebody else, remember this. There could be some poor bugger in that dentist's chair about to get drilled.

Jennifer invites us into their very cosy galley and saloon for tea. Their saloon is heated with the smallest wood stove that I have ever seen. The firewood must have been cut with an electric knife. It is early spring, so the nights on the water are cool; the wood fire looks and smells wonderful. (Can you imagine, they burn cedar wood down there!)

The dentist proceeds to tell us stories of rogue waves and funnel winds that would rip the house off of your boat, currents that suck you into the depths of Davy Jones's locker etc, etc. Why in the hell would he still be on the sea? After he works himself into a frenzy of terror, he leaves us and the boat to walk the dock in an attempt to calm down.

His wife, Jennifer, is sitting in the saloon looking like a poster wife of the 1950's, her hair coiffed, her nail polish matches her shoes and she has on one of those frilly little aprons that my grandma used to wear on special occasions. She exclaims,"Oh my, isn't he just such a snoopy dog! Would you like more tea?" We are sitting with our mouths hanging open, not sure about what happened or what she means by the "snoopy dog" thing.

It turns out that they had extremely bad experiences with the seas in southeast Alaska and this is a ritual for the dentist. Before they left the docks at Ketchikan, he exorcised his demons by visualizing and verbalizing all of the worst possibilities before they set out for the summer. I hope this drama worked for him, it left me with nightmares.

P.S. September 1 is the cutoff day in the U.S. for most of the insurers of recreational boats. This is one of the reasons for the mass exodus of boats to the south, they have to be below Queen Charlotte Sound for their insurance valid after September 1. Besides, the weather just gets miserable. Like the Captain says, "Any fool can cruise the Inside Passage in the summer time. It takes a serious fool to do it in the winter." We resemble that remark.

North To Alaska

ZIMOVIA STRAIGHTS

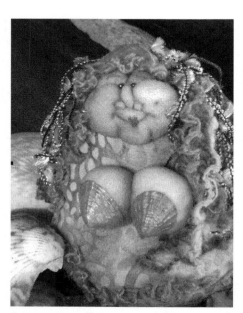

In recognition of his amazing abilities as Captain, I bought "ZIMMIE" as a mascot for the Captain. She has seen us through life and death situations and has kept our heads and hearts out of Davy Jones's locker. Zimmie is short for Zimovia.

The Audrey Eleanor leaves Meyers Chuck, Alaska, early in the afternoon. We had made plans to meet up with the "Jenny" and her crew, the floating dentist and his wife, for cocktails, but the Inn was full. Anchoring looked to be a bit precarious at Meyers Chuck; we felt it was best to head for the next horizon.

Santa Ana Bay looks to be a great place to spend the night; we head north to find out. I can hear a strange sound, zz-zzzz-zzing like razors slicing through material at a high speed...no I have not experienced that, but it's the best way that I can describe it. A very excited Captain yells, "Quick, look portside!"

The ocean is alive, alive with Dall's porpoises. They look like miniature killer whales and they move like lightening. They cut the water so fast that it sounds like electric knives or razors.

This pod (or pods) of porpoises has discovered a school of salmon. There are hundreds of shiny black and white bodies surrounding the boat. The ocean is roiling with porpoises and escaping salmon. It only takes seconds for the eagles and gulls to come screaming in for their share. It's a cacophony of screaming, fighting birds and rolling mammals. On the bow, we have a front row seat and narrowly miss getting whacked in the head by eagles. They are concentrating on stealing what fish they can and nothing else matters.

The gulls come in shrieking a bluff at the eagles and dart back out of claw and slashing beak range in the last second. Porpoises streak through the water and grab air with their catch of salmon flopping desperately in attempts to escape. It's a boiling, roiling, soggy wet dining room.

As quickly as it starts, it ends. The porpoises now have leisure time to digest dinner. They appear to think that we are a large black floating obstacle in their dining room, moving way slower than they are. But what the heck, maybe they can force us to slow down while they digest that lovely salmon and catch a ride in the bow wake of this slow old tub.

This is my first encounter with curious porpoises. I lean over the bow to watch them play in the wake; it's about five feet to the water. They are more curious than I am. A quick flip on their backs and we have eye-to-eye contact. Are they smiling at me? It sure looks like it with their standardized grin.

What to do? Say hello of course, ask how they are doing, would they consider today's catch a good grade of salmon, where are they going to be tomorrow? How's the weather down there…one way conversations run out of steam quickly. As long as I talk to them they stay on their backs, watching me. Any lengthy pause in the conversation and they are gone as quickly as bored teenagers. In a previous story I have mentioned a friend who knows about such things. She said they like female opera singers; I would like to try to play some opera for them to see if this is so.

The porpoises follow us just into the mouth of Santa Ana Bay and they leave. We head further into the cove and pass under double rainbows. This must be a place of magic, to have such an escort and be able to enter through a gateway of rainbows. Where are we?

Santa Ana is a beautiful bay with a fresh water river trickling in at the mouth. At low tide it, is a river that roars. The anchor is dropped and we decide to roar ashore to explore; we do not row, we roar. The last water that we filled the tanks with had been heavily chlorinated, so we are happy to find fresh drinking water. There are fresh bear signs everywhere; this is heavy bush so we don't venture too far from the shore.

As the tide falls, the big round river boulders are exposed. Beautiful indigo mussel shells cover the rocks and sparkle like jewels in the sunshine. There are millions of them blanketing the rocks, ranging in size from barely visible to 6 inches in length. This is heaven; I have to say that I have a weakness for mussels in white wine. Damn reality, or the reality known as the Captain. He tends to be really real sometimes. He points out that we don't know if this area is affected by red tide.

I do know that as a rule May is not a usual time for red tide and these are icy cold waters; do we want to take a chance? Well I suppose not, he volunteers to rub some on his lips to see if there is a reaction (something that he used to do with mushrooms when he was trapping). No, I do not want mussels that badly. Now I wonder why the bears aren't eating the shiny blue mussels. In this land of plenty, only salmon bellies may tempt them with their oily goodness.

Several days later in Wrangell, Alaska, I call the Fish and Wildlife Department to ask about red tide reports. We were going to be travelling in this area for some time so why not find out from the source? The lady on the phone had a very strong south of the border accent. When I asked her about the mussels and the red tide she firstly stated that only the low of the low would eat mussels and as far as the red tide thing went, "When we read 'bout it in the 'bituary" (obituary) we know we got us a problem". Good enough, we know that we are definitely on our own.

By now, you may have noticed that we like to try things that out of the ordinary or off the beaten path. Well, Zimovia Straight is hardly a path.

"God hates a coward" is my Captain's war cry and here we go. The entry isn't too bad and there are range markers dead ahead as I can see with my trusty binoculars. As we get closer to the starboard marker I say to the Captain that they must have had a storm in this area and the marker has been washed up on shore.

The range marker (these are aids to navigation) appears to be in the water along side the bank, the tide is running hard enough that the marker is laying flat with water rooster-tailing up over it. It's decision time, what to do? I am adamant that the marker must have been blown ashore, how on earth could they expect a boat to get that close to the shore and not run aground?

The Captain cranks us hard to portside and behind us over our shoulders is the next marker that we have to have to our starboard side. We head towards this navigation aid, and all of a sudden the depth sounder begins to yell that we have no water underneath our hull. Get out, get out!

Slamming her hard back into reverse the Captain pours the power to our dual engines. The sudden action and full throttle creates a great wake that lifts us off of the shoal. We sheepishly (me mostly) head back toward the shore-bound marker that we needed to stay by in the first place. The Captain has to stop and start to pivot us around the navigation aids in these narrows. At one marker, we had to stop and back up so that we could round the marker. No more narrow escapes, no more second-guessing the markers, no more doubts about the aids of navigation.

Wrangell Narrows was spoken about in our Power Squadron course as being a nerve-wracking challenge. I believe that I counted 64 navigation lights in Wrangell Narrows; it is also known as Christmas Tree Lane. Starboard lights are red and portside lights are green, so the colors alternating all along the narrows do make it feel kind of Christmassy.

After Zimovia, Wrangell Narrows feels like a freeway. After we had finished talking to Fish and Wildlife in Wrangell, we decided to go down to the pub for a beer. Some of the local fishermen were taking a break as well. They asked us if we were off of the old wooden boat and then the usual questions, which way did you come and how was the weather?

When the Captain replied that we had come through Zimovia Straight and that the weather had been wonderful, there was a brief lull in the conversation. One of the older fishermen asked the Captain again, "Did you say Zimovia, son?" (The Captain really liked being referred to as son.)

We had established that this was our first trip on our new old boat and that we were green as grass. The Captain said, "Yes, Zimovia". The fisherman replied, "Well, my boy, you missed a lot of rocks out there, especially in a boat that size, I don't think you can call yourself green no more."

North To Alaska

NUDE OBSERVANCE OF WHALES

"I am glad to have my clothes on." The author, Dawn Kostelnik, at the helm of the Audrey Eleanor, motoring from Juneau, Alaska to Haines, Alaska.

It is a beautiful HOT spring day as we leave Juneau, Alaska, (the capital city of Alaska) heading for Haines on the last leg of our trip to home moorage in Haines. We are crewing our 1948 wooden yacht, the Audrey Eleanor, from Prince Rupert, B.C., Canada.

The sky is a brilliant blue that is matched by the swells on the ocean. Without the snow-tipped mountains as a break it would have been hard to tell where sky ended and sea began. The gentle rolling of the swells is rocking us to sleep as the heat builds; the sun is finally radiating some warmth. The golden rays are penetrating our bodies, wave upon wave of warmth. Equally, layer-by-layer our clothing is coming off; it is finally summer. The flying bridge on Audrey is portioned off from most views by a two and a half foot barrier of blue canvas. If you are lying on the deck on a lounge mat as I am, you cannot be seen by anything less than a cruise ship at close range. There is no chance of that.

The warmth of the sun feels wonderful; my inner core may actually be defrosting after another long winter. Both the Captain and I have little left on in the way of clothing. We are cruising through isolated Alaskan waters. Who would want to sneak up on middle-aged nudists? The Captain is at the helm clad only in his boxers, I think he could remove the hat. I must have dozed off in the comfort of the sun; I wake startled from a deep sleep to, "Starboard, starboard!" I roll over to the rail and pull myself up to take a peek overboard.

A grey humpback whale mom breaks the surface of the sea with a gentle sway of her giant tail; her baby energetically celebrating its new life by jumping for the sun. It circles its mother and leaps skyward "grabbing air" and landing with gigantic baby belly flops. The residual waves are large enough to sink a kayak. This is a good-natured mother. She slows down to allow for the special playtime. You can feel the joy of the baby as he tries again and again to reach the sun.

I am totally focused on the baby whale. My concentration is broken by an evil little chuckle vibrating in the Captain's chest. This is the sound of a deviant. I know this sound, this sound means that somehow I am about to be embarrassed; someway, somehow. Being so absorbed in the whales I hadn't noticed the cruise ship approaching us directly from the bow, it appears to be on top of us. This is one of the smaller ships that offer a more intimate cruising experience. Their experience with the Audrey Eleanor and its crew is way too intimate for my liking.

Whales are now swimming off towards the Icy Straight "aquarium". The happy family is hedging out of view of the binocular-wielding crowd that hangs over the rail of this ship. This little ship sits higher in the water than the Audrey Eleanor does. They will soon have a direct line of sight into our flying bridge. With the whales gone, they are looking for new material to query with their privacy-invading extended eyeballs that hang by black idiot strings from their necks.

My clothes are hanging over the back part of the rail on the opposite side of the deck. I am trying desperately to meld with the blue canvas wall that is my only source of cover from a hundred prying eyes. The passengers are waving enthusiastically at this classic lady (Audrey). As her bow slices through these brilliant blue waters, she creates a magnificent picture. They are probably trying to figure out what that disembodied head is doing crabbing along the rail behind the blue canvas.

The "head" is cursing the laughing Captain, who simply has stepped down into the cockpit; he quite frankly doesn't care who sees him in his underwear. He would not care if he weren't wearing underwear either. They haven't realized that there is a naked, panicked first mate crawling along the deck behind the canvas trying to maintain just a little dignity.

Just as I am deciding that the moment of misery by being exposed while I grab my clothes is possibly minor compared to being pinned-down nude behind the canvas indefinitely, their ship swings to port side; something else has caught their attention, thank goodness. The Captain is howling in glee, I don't like him sometimes.

We are now north of Auke Bay; we had spent three days moored at Douglas Island. At full moon, the tide can rip a bit in front of Juneau. We are in the land of the Midnight Sun, so visually being able to tell if the moon is full or not can be problematic. We appreciate the tide charts.

Approaching Juneau from the south, we had timed our arrival to coincide with the flood tide to make mooring as easy as possible. The wind had been howling and clawing at our backs for days prior to our landing. We tried to raise the Harbour Master as we searched for transit moorage. Call after call goes out, as we get closer to Juneau. No one is coming back on the radio. We pass the U.S. Coast Guard; the crew on board jumps to attention to give us a full salute as we pass. This is an unexpected compliment; the hours of sanding and varnishing are paying off.

Audrey is now in the middle of the boat maze that is the downtown harbour. Still no response on the radio, we will have to back out of this mess. Bowsprits on sailboats turn up as bow-piercing spears where they shouldn't. The Captain is best at backing up. We are back out in the channel that is now a racing tidal river. The tide is ripping and the wind is whipping up water as it pushes and shoves against the running tide. We head for safe moorage at Douglas Island.

The response we have been waiting for on the radio now comes through.

"Hey, are you guys in that classic old boat? Would love to see her close up, sorry no moorage, we are moving boats out right now, try Douglas Island!"

Douglas Island is on our starboard side, it's difficult to see the entrance to the marina. There is a long rock wall that appears to run in a continuous line, we can't see the opening into the harbour. The Captain does not have the luxury of taking his time; the tide is running hard so we have to go in under full power. He swings us blindly and hard to starboard; common sense dictates that there has to be an opening at the southern point of the rock wall. We can see sailboat masts behind the wall, but where?

YES! Right in front of us is the rather small opening. It may only seem very tiny as we arrive under full power backed up by 30 tonnes. I am standing on the bow with the ropes ready; I hate this part of mooring. There is a 4 foot drop from Audrey's bow to any surface. Sometimes there are rails on the docks, sometimes giant cleats and in Petersburg, Alaska, there is a solid length of pipe to secure your lines to. I landed on that pipe once; it really hurt. There is no one else, I AM THE CREW! I ready myself for the jump to the dock and prepare to secure our lines.

Looming up suddenly and directly in front of me is a solid steel pillar. We are on a collision course with direct and immediate impact. 30 tonnes of ship will not slow down in this limited amount of space and time. I drop and flatten to the deck; I can visualize my toes clawing through my shoes trying to anchor me to the strips of teak on the deck of the Audrey Eleanor. I see me splatted against the steel pillar and sliding down into the water in classic Road Runner style. I wait for the impact…and wait. Time has changed into slow motion and impact doesn't happen.

Looking up I can see a man and woman standing on the dock watching this performance, I jump to my feet and throw them the rope in a flash, they quickly tie us up. After taking a deep breath I look around trying to figure out what has happened. The Alaskan fisherman on the dock yells, "Man that was some bad assed boat driving!"

Audrey has her nose stuck into a 25 foot slip leaving 30 feet of her aft end blocking the entrance to the rest of the marina; the Captain looks a little pale. My eyes query him, "How did you do that?" He simply shakes his head. The Harbour Master shows up, he has an amused look on his face.

"I'm sure you know that you'll have to move your boat," he says. "You are kinda blocking the harbour."

I can see that he's having difficulty keeping his laughter under control. The Captain says, "I think I should sit up on the top deck and have a beer before I do anything."

The Harbour Master is a great guy, he throws us the keys to his car and says, "You might want to go into Juneau and buy a whole case."

We had use of his car for the three days that we were there.

North To Alaska

BEHIND SULLIVAN ISLAND

Our friends from Texas, Lubor and Tena, lounge on the flying bridge of the Audrey Eleanor; Captain, Rick Cousins is in the background. We are leaving Sullivan Island.

For a quick escape into the wilder, wilderness of Alaska aboard the "speed demon" Audrey Eleanor, it takes approximately 2 hours and is roughly 30 kilometres. We love to cruise behind Sullivan Island, south of Haines, Alaska, and swing on the hook for few days of solitude.

The warmth of friends who came along for the ride enhances memories of these excursions; they were all shanghaied as willing crews. David brought his guitar and sang ballads about the Yukon and Northern B.C. that he had written himself. My favourite is still the one about being "up behind the mine in Faro". Where's the C.D., David?

On this particular trip, we have a large stash of fireworks aboard. Shooting off fireworks in the northern summer has always been a bit of a conundrum to me. I think the fireworks that we shoot off on July 1 could be saved for the winter so that we can actually see them. Fireworks are visual; it is supposed to be visual, is it not? The venue changes if you are sitting in a harbour that is encased in huge, snow-capped mountains. These create a perfect backdrop and reflector of sound, these mammoth stone walls create the perfect platform for an echo, an echo, an echo, echo.

David and Don go ashore to light the entertainment. Diane, Jean, and I sit on the flying bridgem waiting to see what the results will be. It is June in the land of the Midnight Sun after all, a summer solstice month. The Captain is on the bow with the binoculars, watching the whole procedure.

"It's lit," he calls, and even with our naked eyes we can see the little puff of smoke on the beach. A thin trail of smoke follows the tiny, tiny light that straggles into the sky and dies out with a disappointingly small bang. A collective breath escapes the audience. Oh well, we have all had this experience before.

But what is that? An echo begins to build in the mountains. It sounds like a gunshot in the distance as it rolls around the mountain rim and grows in volume. The little bang has grown in strength and begins to echo back and forth between the rock walls. This is very interesting, now the fireworks do have some entertainment value. The guys are excited as they set off a combination of rockets.

Sounds start small and grow with a crescendo of deep booms. Bursts of staccato gunfire shots engulf us. We are yelling in excitement but can't hear each other. The vibrations are felt through the deck and climb the legs of our chairs. This is the three dimensional effect that Disney has been trying to duplicate. Round after round of fireworks rattle the chairs. We are sure that they must hear it in Haines and are preparing for the much-anticipated invasion of terrorists we keep hearing about from our southern neighbours. The homeland security gang wasn't here this weekend, thank goodness.

The pyro crew climbs back into the zodiac on the beach, and we can barely see them for the gunpowder smoke. A distant echo reaches further and further, and finally climbs back over the last mountain. We are silent; shadows of the thunder from the rockets are still reverberating in our empty cranial chambers. Sound, loud sound, empties the mind. With a great sigh, the top level of silence is broken. David will have to sing his heart out to top that…he does.

Tides in Alaska are stronger and much larger than in Texas. The Texans would never agree to that, but it is reality. Friends of ours from Texas will have to attest to that. Lubor and Tena wanted to go ashore to explore the Alaskan wilderness. The zodiac and kicker are heavy; you can sort of drag them along the beach if there are no barnacles or such to tear and rip out the bottom of the rubber boat. On a wet tidal beach, the boat sucks down deep into the muck and it is impossible to get it to move without removing the kicker. When we told them about the tide, I believe that they thought that nothing could be bigger then anything in Texas. This simply wasn't possible or the concept didn't register. They teach them that in Texas, you know.

The Captain and I stayed aboard to clean up and reorganize and to let the couple have a bit of a run-away. They often visit the Yukon and Alaska to recharge and escape the crazy pressures of life in Houston, Texas. Sometimes in day-to-day conversation with our friends, I wonder how they survived their lifestyle in that wasp's nest. They, in turn, could not understand our priorities. I only know that if I wanted to relax and regroup, I wouldn't be going to Texas to do it.

This couple would show up in Whitehorse stretched to the limit and looking like they could not spend another day in their world. When it was time for them to leave, the light was back in their eyes and their souls were recharged. I often wondered what would happen if they just stayed, simply stepped out of their other life in the big city. What type of people would they become with all the material fluff removed from their lives? I wanted them to know that most of us already knew about that "other" life and we had chosen to leave it behind. We chose to be Northerners.

The tide rises 26 feet some days, and it drops 26 feet some days. Today was one of those days. They caught it about half-way out and pulled the zodiac on the beach so it wouldn't leave. This was very thoughtful for sure. With the tide going out though, getting the zodiac back to water was going to be HARD! After a leisurely walk on the beach, they returned to find themselves with the zodiac high and dry. Tena is not a very strong lady, and the weight for Lubor to pull alone was simply too much. They tugged and pulled and made no headway.

We can see a momma grizzly and three babies off in the distance. Now we are feeling a little excited. We don't want to scare these southern people just yet. Lubor removes the kicker and heads towards the ocean. He doesn't set it close enough to the water, I'm sure he is considering that the tide should now return… it would be, in Texas. He returns to the zodiac and without the weight of the kicker he and Tena can now drag the zodiac to the water. The water is now further past where the kicker is set. The zodiac is left at the water's edge and the whole procedure is repeated, a few times over. They start their return to Audrey exhausted.

In the meantime, momma grizzly and the three cubs have gotten to the spot where the initial parking of the zodiac took place. Momma is agitated because from the opposite end of the beach a big black bear boar is approaching her and her family on a collision course. Plus, she can smell humans on her beach. We watch from on board, the Captain with his hand on his rifle. Our two Texans are rowing toward the boat unaware of this whole other drama going on; we never did tell them.

Tena must have had an extra sense about the whole thing though. She stayed on board the next day and was sitting on the flying bridge in 27° C sunshine with her jacket on. She kept trying to call out on her cell phone, finally in frustration she yelled, "The damned thing won't work, what am I going to do?"

I told her that it was unlikely that the cell would work behind this island and that was one of the great things about this area, NO CELL SERVICE! Life slows down when you get rid of the cell phone. She gave me a variety of reasons why she had to stay connected. The reasons were all rationalized away. When the truth finally showed its naked face there really was not much I could say.

"Well when the bears swim out to attack us, how can I call 911?" she blurted.

The Captain had his first hummingbird experience behind Sullivan Island. No, this is not code for something else. Hummingbirds move so quickly that it's hard to see them the first time, especially against the water. I am trying to explain to my hard of hearing Captain what they sound like, not a chance. In the state of Michoacán, Mexico, there is an ancient archaeological site with a village called Zinzunzan. These ancient peoples named the village after the sound that a hummingbird makes.

My Captain is lying on the front deck, shirtless in the sunshine; I am climbing up from inside the saloon and call to him. He sits up just as a hummingbird decides to check out this strange flower.

There they are. The hummingbird suspended in mid-flight with his needle-like beak, maybe an inch away from the Captain's beak. They both try to focus on their opposing obstacles to no avail.

I can't tell if the hummingbird is cross-eyed, but the Captain sure is. The hummingbird gives up trying to figure out this cross-eyed flower and whirls (zinzunzan) off into the sunshine. Now the Captain knows what hummingbirds sound like...and look like.

P.S. Lubor, now you know, the "Rest of The Story."

North To Alaska

AUDREY'S LIFE AS WE KNOW IT

The Audrey Eleanor in Skagway, Alaska.

With four years of the Adventures of The Audrey Eleanor appearing in the Whitehorse Star on a bi-monthly basis, more and more people want to know more about "her" and the future of the series. The Whitehorse Star is a century-old newspaper that serves both the Yukon and parts of Alaska.

What is she, The Audrey Eleanor (make and model), where did she come from and where did we get her name? Some of the other questions I refuse to answer, except yes, the Captain is a happy man and no, I do not do dishes for anyone else. Yes, we believe that Audrey still loves us as much as we love her.

With regards to the book that I promised, this is a struggle for me. I have reorganized The Adventures of the Audrey Eleanor and put them in chronological order and finished up to chapter seven. It was a chore,

I don't expect much of anything to be easy, but this was grinding. I lost all of my passion in the process of the "chore." There was no life to it and it was terrible. My solution is to do this website and give you my very best. A compilation in the form of the book could appear once the website and Kobo (a Canadian e-publisher) page have been finished, and here it is!

I attended a writers conference in Puerto Vallarta in February, 2012. I do have publishers that would publish the book once I get it structured and present a completed manuscript to them. I caught the eye of an extremely credible agent from New York while I was there flogging my wares. She wants me to fictionalize my work; risk of liability runs high in the publishing world. I may do this once I have finished my current project.

I met an amazing gentleman from Texas; his name is Caleb Pirtle III, founding partner of Venture Galleries. I invited him to the Yukon, suggesting that he participate in our Great Northern Story Telling Festival. I hope he can contact the Great Northern Story Telling Festival, I haven't been able to.

Mr. Pirtle is my father's age. He suggested to me that it was time I jumped into the current technological century and realize where the publishing world is headed. A conclusion of the writers conference was that the published world as we know it is currently standing on its head and who knows where it will end up; the industry certainly doesn't. Things are moving faster and faster, the need for stories that are concise, short and sweet is on the rise. The birth of www.thewhitegirl.ca is a result of that conversation. I hope you enjoy the site.

We had toyed with the idea of doing charters onboard the Audrey Eleanor, but have since discarded the idea. An old proverb states: fish and friends have this in common, after three days they start to smell bad. Man, when I first wrote those lines it caused a kerfuffle. It was even discussed in the "other" newspaper by indignant people within their own articles and columns.

But once again, we really like our friends and don't want to smell bad to them within any timeframe. The concept of a Boat and Breakfast really appealed to us. At one point we had enormous support from people in Powell River, B.C, to do just that.

It would take a mountain of money to bring Audrey back to her old standard, but it would have been a worthwhile investment with the prospects of a business behind it. It only takes one bad bureaucrat to spoil a whole concept and sometimes a whole town. I am tired, I don't want yet another fight with narrow-minded officials. We shelved that idea...for now.

Getting back to the Audrey Eleanor. The Derbyshire family of Kent, Washington, commissioned a skilled shipwright named Otto Ranft to build their dream yacht in 1946. Mr. Ranft had been crafting award-winning speed and race boats in Puget Sound and Portland, Oregon, for more than 40 years.

The Derbyshires gave him their specifications, but also gave him free rein. This would be his dream yacht as well: she would also be the biggest ship that he ever built.

Construction began high up on a hill in a cherry orchard overlooking Kent. The ship was then known as the "Tilly Dee." Mr. Ranft emphasized that no nails were used; the yacht was screw-fastened and plugged.

Her L.O.A. (length over all) is 54 feet with a 13.6 foot beam and headroom of 6 feet 3 inches. The hull is yellow cedar and fir on a laminated oak frame. At the time, her staterooms were carpeted in blue velvet; there were handmade nautical curtains made of white duck at the windows.

"The furniture and interior is all of mahogany. Finished in pale turquoise with mahogany trim, the staterooms are just beautiful."

This is a direct quote from the local Kent newspaper on July 9, 1948, when she was being launched from the Boeing plant in Renton, Washington.

My galley has a 1947 dishwasher in it that still works. I did not realize that they made them back then.

She was powered with twin Chryslers and hit a top speed of 22 knots. Can you imagine being passed by a 54 foot wooden boat that weighs 30 tonnes? It must have been one hell of a wake! Otto Ranft specialized in speedboats, and she is a big one. I have to tell you that today we think we flying when we hit 14 knots.

It was her hull design that caught the attention of the CYA (Classic Yacht Association) in Nanaimo, B.C. If you check their website she may still be there: www.classicyacht.org.

The cost of construction in 1948 was $45,000.00. With inflation, it would cost $428,571.43 to build her today. Most of the finishing wood used in her construction then is now either a protected or extinct species. It is not likely that she could ever be duplicated.

As with any grand, old, and "interesting" lady, there are dark whispers and sordid stories about her colourful past. Any person with character acquires their experience somewhere, and usually not from following normal procedure.

When we re-registered her in Canada from Alaska, she was still known as the "Fluid Tite" in the Victoria registry. The owner of that era manufactured hydraulic fittings. While I appreciate the opportunity this presented him to use the yacht as a tax write-off, the name "Fluid Tite" is one that I preferred to live without.

She was also known as the "Lady Evans" when Senator Walter Evans from Washington State purchased her. There was an old orange life ring etched with faded lettering, "The Lady Evans", on board when we first bought her.

That story goes that there was a conflict regarding the payment of duty when she was first brought into Canadian waters by the U.S. Senator. He did not want to pay the duty. Apparently, the customs agents found The Lady Evans, as she was known, aboard a railway car bound for Lake Winnipeg. Do you suppose they would launch her in Lake Winnipeg and she would not be noticed??

Audrey Eleanor is a bit of a show-off, so I don't understand how they figured that this ruse would work. Before she could slip away, clacking down the rail tracks into the dark of the night, she was seized by the Internal Revenue guys (surely otherwise known as Ring Wraiths) and the Senator died during the lengthy court battle that followed.

Audrey is almost 65 years old. For 63 of those years, she has run between Alaska in the north and California in the south. Some stories we can verify; lots we can't. I have collected information from the Vancouver Maritime Museum where Audrey spent some time on display in their harbour.

The Maritime Museum has extended an open invitation for Audrey (the Senator 11) to return to the museum for moorage. Moorage rates in Vancouver require big bucks; this invitation to moor dockside at the museum and allow people to walk on the dock beside us in exchange for reasonable moorage is most appreciated.

I have a faded copy of the Kent newspaper with the story of her launching. Other information comes from past owners who verbally, and with logbooks, have passed along valuable history.

Audrey was fully restored between 1981 and 1984 in Richmond, B.C. Four doctors bought and restored her. They then christened her the Senator 11 (after the Senator who died during the battle with CRA), but did not officially register her as such. There is a lengthy procedure to re-christen a ship without branding her with bad luck; such concepts as breaking champagne on her bow and having a virgin pee on the decks…such fun.

I was fortunate enough to talk to Dr. Carl Whitesides, a previous owner. After all of these years, he was in love with her still. He wanted to know if there was an occasional drip above the Captain's berth. I was able to assure him that it was there, it's on my side of the berth and it hits me in the forehead.

When we bought the Audrey Eleanor in 2003, she was still known as the Senator 11. The previous owners had bought her as a wedding present for themselves. Blake and Amy Dewhurst then made the Senator 11 their home for 5 years. She was moored in McLean's Shipyard for almost 10 years; this is one of the oldest working shipyards in B.C., and this is where we finally found her.

North to Alaska, words that set Johnny Horton singing in my head. We wanted to bring our lady closer to home, which is Whitehorse, Yukon Territory, Canada. The closest Harbour to Whitehorse is located in Skagway, Alaska, but we preferred the quiet and quaint fishing village of Haines, Alaska. Our maiden voyage took us from Prince Rupert, B.C., Canada, to Haines. We were a green, green crew of two, such stories I have to tell you!

To put this into perspective…the M.V. Anna Maria is 65 feet in length. She left the Yukon and Alaska with a crew of six experienced seamen to crew her down to southern B.C. We are 54 feet in length and we are a new crew of two. A little knowledge is indeed dangerous; we came armed with a navigation course from the Canadian Power Squadron and felt totally confident that we could deal with anything! Good work guys.

By the way, people, you need to understand and know both tide and current tables. There is not much of a call for current tables in the north, and it becomes a huge health hazard in the south. Ignorance can kill you.

"God hates a coward!" My Captain's war cry.

The thought of failing never crossed our minds. Sinking perhaps, but never failing. Failing would have been not trying at all. Lots of you were onboard the Audrey Eleanor while she was moored in Haines, so you know that we survived our maiden voyage, but it really was only by the hair of our chinny-chin-chins.

The name Audrey Eleanor comes from the Captain's mom, Audrey Eleanor Cousins, née Church. It is always a difficult choice when you are naming something so significant. There are many versions of the name Dawn flaunted across the bows of M.V.'s...Morning Dawn, Pacific Dawn...

My mom's name is Patricia Dawn. I wanted something a little different for our ship.

Audrey Eleanor Cousins is a lady who raised 12 children. Five came with the daddy as a package deal and then she birthed seven more of her own. She was still cutting firewood at the age of 83 and took care of old people well into her seventies. At the age of 64 she went back to university and graduated at 69 while caring for an aging husband with Alzheimer's. I wanted that type of tenacity under my feet at we crashed through waves.

The Audrey Eleanor is currently registered in Victoria as the Audrey Eleanor 1 with her port of registry being Whitehorse, Yukon Territory. We have been told that there are two M.V.s registered out of Whitehorse, and we wonder...who you are?

Cries of the Furies

FROM ALASKA TO
DEEP BAY, BC

Find the full map here:

http://thewhitegirl.ca/stories/audrey-eleanor-map

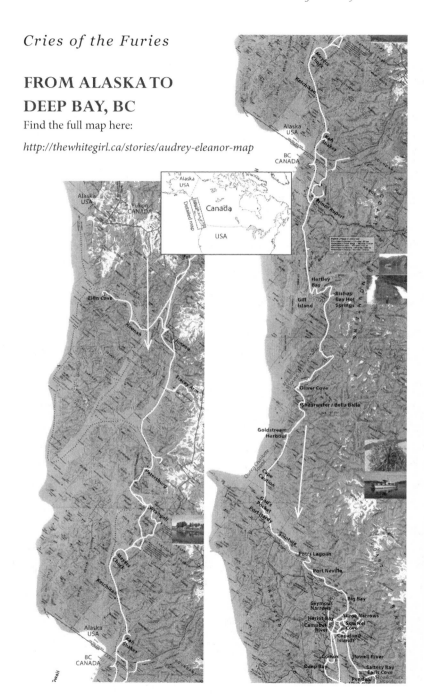

Cries of the Furies

A SLEEPING GIANT

A grey whale snoozes beside the Audrey Eleanor; the clank of the anchor wakes him and with a single graceful sway of his tail, he moves on.

Audrey pulled away from her moorage in Haines, Alaska, on July 26, 2006. Haines was difficult to leave; we'd established wonderful friendships on the docks and in the community as well. Richard from the Eleanor S would no longer commission us to spy on his daughter; she sometimes spent the night onboard the Eleanor S. He wanted to know whom she was holding hands with. She prepared her own reports for us to pass along to Richard, her vigilant father.

Carl off of Driftwood Charters had married Jenny and was no longer perusing Canadian girls. We had enjoyed many dungeness crab fests at his little house, tucked into the Alaskan wilderness with an outlook over Mud Bay. While we ate, he quizzed us on available Whitehorse women. His honesty was refreshing; Carl was looking for a wife. Not a maid or a nurse, but a wife who would be his partner during his life.

He had criteria to follow and was direct in his approach. Jenny ended up being his lady.

This does not remind me of Carl, but it jumps into my mind as part of the usual gyrations of northern romance. I am reminded of a time when my brother Joel and I were in Haines, years ago. He was chatting up the barmaid and asked what had brought her to Alaska. Her reply, "the men". His eyes lit up at the response. When he asked if she had been successful in her search she replied, "The odds are good and the goods are odd." I laughed for days over this.

Judy, from the homebuilt ship the Arcturus, gave us her personal copy of a book that she wrote on edible plants in Alaska. The University of Alaska was in the process of having it published; it supplied us with invaluable information on edible plants and seaweed in Alaska. I developed a fondness for sea asparagus.

B.J. McLean from Whitehorse donated a copy of her CD "January Thaw". I'm not sure if it helped with the homesickness or made it worse… it sings of our Yukon home and is still one of our favourites. B.J.'s songs bring the northern night skies and friendships crawling up onto your lap anywhere that you go. She suggested that the Captain pay particular attention to the "Plump and Friendly Northern Girl" song. He loved flirting with her.

My brother Kurtis had decided that we needed an escort from Haines to at least Hoonah, Alaska. Kurtis uses ANY reason to escape to the sea. Our escort grew to include my parents, Rick's youngest daughter, Alanah, Kurt's wife Janine and my little niece Jianna Mia, who was five months old at the time. Jianna is a very special little girl; we waited for her for 10 years. She finally arrived after her parents spent a most wonderful long weekend boating in Alaska. Mia her middle name, and it stands for Made in Alaska.

We end up dropping the hook behind Sullivan Island the first day out; our 8 knots couldn't outrun the weather we ran into alongside Eldred Rock. The next afternoon, we motored into Hoonah, Yukon. That is not a typo; there were more Yukoners on the transient dock than Alaskans. The flying bridge on Audrey is a most social place. The Captain deep-fried fresh halibut on the back deck and the fishing stories on the bridge grew as the pinks and purples of the summer night sky reflected back at us in the glass-calm water.

Fishing in Hoonah! For some of us in the north, this is what summer is! Icy Straight is thick with marine life; salmon jump out of the water, saying pick me, look at me, pick me. I know, I know, I've heard the sea lice theory, but I prefer mine. People say that Icy Straight is a living aquarium and I agree. Kurtis heads out to scout out the fishing ground. We are the mother ship, most meals are done aboard Audrey and the jolly jumper is easy entertainment for Jianna and us as well. A little wake action winds up the jolly jumper and gets that baby swinging in all directions.

At 8 knots (approximately 10 mph) we get to see a lot of things that I suspect a person misses at 20+ mph. Porpoises love our bow wake, they ride it and roll and race each other. If you lie on the bow and hang your head over the edge, they roll over and make eye contact. They will continue to stay in the wake with eye contact as long as you can carry on an ANIMATED conversation with them. It's harder than it sounds, a one-way conversation with a marine mammal runs out of steam quickly. What to say to a porpoise? A friend of mine who knows these things says very loud female opera keeps them fascinated for half an hour at a time... I have yet to try.

We catch up with Kurtis at the fishing ground, anchors are set, fishing lines are baited with squid and dropped, and the games have begun. Once the engines are cut, the quiet drops down off of the mountains and the sea sings its song. We are surrounded and serenaded by choruses of whale song. Their calls pulse deep through the black water and resonate in our bones. In their world, even in a large boat, we are comparatively very, very small. Thank goodness they tolerate us and allow our intrusion into their life. The sonar and depth-sounders are silenced, these waves can kill sea life, especially whales. Turn off your sonar around sea life!

The whale songs remind me of when I was a child. I would swing a piece of garden hose through the air for the sound effect; it's a close second to the sound of these humpback whales. I touch Audrey's hull and the vibration of their songs carries through the wood and into my hands and vibrates to the tips of my fingers. I have contact.

The majority of the halibut we are catching are chickens, (roughly 40 lbs and less) and in my opinion the best eating. I tell our boys at moose hunting season, you don't eat the antlers; try to shoot a nice young bull. The smaller the horns, the younger the animal and the better the meat.

With some of the big old bulls, I believe that the horns would be better eating than the tough old critters they came from. I believe that the same applies to halibut. Mercury levels in fish rise as the age of them increases; the longer the time frame of growth, the more the toxins accumulate in the flesh of the fish.

With all of our concentration focused on hauling in halibut, we don't notice that a sleeping giant has slipped quietly into the neighbourhood.

One by one we notice our visitor. We need to pay attention and pull in our fishing lines. Everyone tiptoes and whispers as we edge closer to the port side of the boat. There, a few feet from the gunnels, is an incredible sight, a sleeping whale. This giant male is suspended beside us in the sea and is very close to the same size as the Audrey Eleanor. We are in awe, we whisper to each other in amazement. Then we begin to worry, he hasn't moved for a long time. Is he hurt, or possibly dead?

We've never seen a sleeping whale before. The whale is drifting with the tide. It is getting closer and closer to the Audrey Eleanor. The Captain decides that we need to pull anchor, if the whale wakes and is startled we don't know how he will react. One quick flick of his gigantic tail could be the end of us all. We have been told that the few disastrous whale encounters have usually been while they are asleep or they are startled out of sleep. The clank of the chain and anchor wake him and with no effort he moves his colossal tail and leaves us to wonder.

The Captain now begins to wonder about his crew. I have put Audrey in reverse and begin to slowly back away…holy shit! Our day's catch of halibut is tied under the swim grid off the aft deck. I cut the engines quickly and we all rush to see what kind of damage has been done. The screws (propellers) have perfectly cut off the tail of one fish and slightly chewed the tail of another. Tonight's supper is intact and I am singing with whales, hallelujah!

Elfin Cove is located on the northwestern corner of Chichagof Island, west of Juneau, Alaska. This is just on the outside edge of the Inside Passage, still in fairly protected waters, the outer edge leads Straight to Japan. We have been told repeatedly that our boat will not be able to navigate the narrow and shallow dredged channel that leads into the protected inner harbour of Elfin Cove.

"God hates a coward" is what the Captain responds with, his war cry. Audrey is soon safely secured to the dock in Elfin Cove, in the inner harbour.

What is this place? We have entered another world. Crooked little houses in bright colours hang off of rocky cliffs. Flowers are being grown in anything that will hold dirt: an old boot, hollowed out log, rusty teapots sprout beautiful blooms. There are no cars or trucks, there are no roads! Boardwalk webs connect house to house and house to dock. Fly here or boat here; lack of access keeps the crowds down in this place of magic. Halibut are caught off of the dock, still. Who could have discovered this tiny harbour tucked into this remote island? What a jewel was uncovered with the discovery of this tiny harbour, the first explorers must have been elated to discover this magical space.

Monsoons in Alaska. Ask anyone who has boated here and they will verify the truth of this. Tonight it is pouring, a deluge. Our 32-volt chest freezer onboard is loaded with the last few days' catch of halibut. Dinner is in the saloon of the Audrey Eleanor; packed wall to wall with steaming people, our house lights slowly fade and are becoming dim. The heat from the oil-fired Dickinson stove in the galley is competing with the chill and wet of this downpour, setting off its own clouds of condensation. Lights are fading into black and it is getting harder and harder to see. We think it's from the steam of soggy people, but begin to realize that the lights are dimming from some other sinister reason.

Power is being lost. Oh no, the freezer is full of everyone's halibut, how long will they stay frozen? Salmon and crab cakes are forgotten as everyone throws their solution in the melting pot of ideas. On board one of the fish boats is the electrical repair guy, he knows nothing about a 32-volt system. He recalls that his grandfather had one on his fishing boat, but that's the extent of that. By process of elimination, the Captain has narrowed the solution down to; we need to go to Juneau for parts, quickly, before the fish thaw.

Kurtis heads over to Pelican Cove the next afternoon, we have to wait for flood tide to leave the inner harbour. Audrey and the crew make waves for Juneau, possibly Hoonah. Old systems can be fixed; this is why we have maintained our 32-volt system. Overall it mostly works and if it doesn't, replacement parts can either be found or made. Basic mechanics put things right again. 32-volt light bulbs are expensive; on the other hand, I have not had to replace a bulb in years.

We experience our first real ocean swell as we leave Elfin Cove. Open to Russia and Japan, the sea rolls into the mouth of Icy Straight. Swells are telling you that there is a storm out on the open ocean somewhere distant. Pay attention, it could be coming your way. Swells warn you to take cover on the inside. As fast as our 8 knots can go, we are heading to Hoonah. The rise and the fall of the great swells underneath us is exhilarating, this is fun. It makes it difficult to see the whales.

Great greys are slapping giant tails on the ocean; they breach and fall back into the mighty sea with huge waves that ripple mini tsunamis. These giant whales are in their home element. Dall's porpoises zip in rings around each other, looking like baby killer whales; they remind me of puppies chasing each others' tails. I love their grace and ease as they slice through the water with smiles on their porpoise faces. I now realize the reasons that salmon begin to spring in the air for no apparent reason; someone underneath them wants them for dinner. They are trying to escape.

Manoeuvring parts of this and bits of that, the Captain has managed to coax the compressor on the fridge and freezer to produce cold again. With the freezer crammed to capacity, the halibut maintained its temperature, so no spoiled fish.

P.S. The morning that we finally left Hoonah, I woke to find an incredible gift sitting on the back deck. Richard Boyce's daughter that we were supposed to be spying on in Haines was in Icy Straight commercial halibut fishing with her father…she left me a giant barnacle as a going away present. The size of it is hardly believable. Almost two years later we ran into her in La Paz, Mexico. She was working as 3rd mate onboard the "Sea Lion", a National Geographic ship that was doing exploration work in the Sea of Cortez. You just never know, where are you now, Lucy?

Cries of the Furies

TRACY ARM: CHANNEL OF ICEBERGS

Nosing into the rocky shoreline, I am to fill our water jugs with this wildly fresh water

Word has gotten out that Tracy Arm rivals Glacier Bay for magnificent glaciers and stunning scenery. The ice walls cave and collapse into the ocean with a force that creates huge, resounding waves. Waves tinkle the neon blue icebergs like giant ice cubes, mingling like new friends in a crystal glass. This solid granite canyon must have been created when the earth experienced an extreme upheaval and the rock cracked like a hard-boiled egg to expose wide white bands of contrasting colour that offset the milky green water. This is the ultimate in exterior design.

Tracy Arm is south of Juneau, Alaska, by approximately 50 kilometres. Icebergs ranging from barely noticeable (bergies) to spectacular glistening jewels guard the entrance to Tracy Arm. Navigation is difficult, because the ice can obscure the range markers at the entrance, or solid blue crystals block the pathway. "Bergs of bergies" do not move readily.

At low tide the whole procedure becomes quite interesting as swirls and tidal rips develop in the sea and mountains of ice sway in the current and are intent on blocking your route…while we have had to do some tricky navigating to get inside, it is worth it.

Traffic has increased since we first explored this channel; the cruise ships now navigate the rock canyons. Depending on the year, the icebergs can limit your access up the 30 kilometres channel and, of course, tides affect everything.

We are making our way south this time and cannot resist trying once again to get a look at the Sawyer Glacier. A past attempt to reach the end of the arm and see the glacier had been thwarted by a flotilla of icebergs at the 10 kilometre range. The tides aren't running in our favour this time either, but what the heck, and as I'm sure you know by now, "God hates a coward!"

The anchor gets dropped in the little bay in the mouth of the arm. There are several boats here this time. A 45 foot sailboat has been tied to the trees along the shore and looks to be about 4 feet away from the sheer rock edge. It is difficult to anchor with a combination of baby icebergs and boats, all crowding for the limited space. This is quite a difference from the last time we visited, when we were the sole occupants of the cove. From my galley window, I can see a little iceberg that's attempting to rub shoulders with Audrey. It's fairly small and is floating, so no worries. The little iceberg needs to worry; the Captain has decided that he wants to fill the ice coolers with berg ice. This ice is compressed, ancient and lasts way longer than any ice we can buy or make. It makes such a beautiful blue contrast against red crab.

We are a few days from Petersburg and will stock up on king crab when we get there. By stock up, I mean we will eat all that we can and get a whole live one for the road. Any seafood is better when it's fresh, so our philosophy is to catch it as we need it or flag down the commercial boats to see if they are able to sell or trade their catch. The prawn fishers seem to prefer swapping prawns for beer rather than cash. This barter system is often preferred, fresh bread goes almost as far as beer, but not quite.

Seafood is so delicate, and it takes no time before it acquires a freezer flavour that reduces it to mystery fish. Hmm are you sure that this is halibut? Tastes like salt cod! How much do two people really need? I would like to come back tomorrow and still be able to get king crab. Leave the big guys for reproduction and throw the little guys back so they can grow up.

The little "berg" is roped to the side of the boat and the Captain hacks away at crystals of brilliant blue. He passes me one of the bigger chunks to feel; it is heavier than regular ice.

In the morning, a huge cruise ship is leaving the Arm. We wait for the ice to quit moving from their wake before we head up the channel. The tide is returning, so we are following the bergs into the Arm. We hope that we have enough time before the tide changes and we have to fight our way against the ice.

On a little rock ledge, there is a momma bear with this year's cubs hiding between her legs. It's a straight drop into the ocean below if they slip. We are not sure of what she is trying to accomplish and she's looking a little uncertain herself. Audrey slows down and we stay far enough away from her so we don't add to the confusion.

With a roar, a thirty foot tour boat comes out of nowhere. The idiot pilot stops his boat right under the bears and cameras click like typewriters gone berserk…the poor bears scatter up the cliff. The babies are bawling in fear with the whites in their eyes showing in terror. They are slipping and falling, we fully expect to see one of them drop the 20 feet into the ocean. The Captain is furious, if we would have found anything on board to throw at this stupid tour operator, it would have happened

The tour boat hits full throttle again and roars off around the corner, leaving the rest of us to deal with the ice banging against our hulls from the wake they've created. The bears shoot dirty looks over their shoulders as they top the 60 foot cliff; obviously they are glad to be done with all of us. I can see momma bear muttering, "Some people's children, no manners at all!"

Our necks are cramping from looking skyward up the straight flat rock that heads straight up to the sun and drops directly below the surface of the ocean. With the sheer drop into the ocean, the depth of the water allows for some unusual boating. Waterfalls cascade down the rock all around us, spilling beautiful crystal clear glacier water into the sea.

The Captain brings Audrey's bow toward the shoreline between two waterfalls. I am on the bow, not sure what he is doing. He slowly inches us forward until our bow is touching the sheer rock face between the two falls. This is so out of the realm of usual that my instincts are on full alert.

We're too close to the rock, we're too close to the rock. What comes out my mouth is, "What in the hell are you doing?"

He laughs, puts Audrey in neutral and throws me the water jug. "You've always wanted to take a shower under a waterfall" he says, "I expect by the time that the jug is only partially full, you will be soaking wet."

I cannot back down because this is true, I do mange to fill the jug AND stay fairly dry. It's an incredible feeling being underneath tons of falling water with mist blowing around you, I would love to do it again, in warmer water! This liquid ice will be great for drinking and it makes exceptional coffee.

Around the corner under full throttle cruises the "Empress of the North". She's a replica of an old riverboat complete with fake waterwheel. If you glitzed up the SS Klondike in Whitehorse, Yukon, she would be a smaller twin. Her hull is smashing through the ice and we wonder if she's been reinforced as an icebreaker. We have seen her several times before, her passengers always seem the happiest of the cruisers. They hang over the sides and wave and shout as they go by. Lots of the other cruise ship passengers don't respond to a friendly wave. Everyone is heading for the glacier.

A small thump resonates a vibration through the hull, then a bigger one and a bigger vibration. We are two kilometres from the glacier, but the tide has turned and now the icebergs are bumping against our hull. It is amazing how little "give" there is in a floating block of ice. I'd assumed that our bow wake would simply push the ice to the side; that isn't what happens. The little ones will move. By little I mean no bigger than three feet in diameter, after that it's like hitting a rock wall. Sitting still, we can feel the ice hitting the hull, causing vibrations through Audrey's bones. It's time to back out of here. The ice is packing quickly, so we do have to back up to get out of the icepack. Again, so close and yet so far. Next time, we'll make it.

P.S. The Empress of the North has a record of running aground at least once a year. She ran aground again shortly after we saw her and was out of commission for the rest to the season. Whatever they are doing they seem to have the most fun while they are afloat.

Cries of the Furies

MICE IN THE HICE

The galley on board the Audrey Eleanor, headquarters for stowaways!

We are docked in Prince Rupert, B.C. It feels great to be back in Canadian waters. Audrey has been de-registered in record time, thanks to Sheila (she is amazing), and we are once again Canadian-registered with our home port being Whitehorse, Yukon Territory. We were never boarded by the U.S. homeland security, but the threat was always there like a heavy, very oppressive weight hovering over our bow. There is something about 18 year old boys with 50 calibre machine guns at their disposal that makes us really nervous. (This was the homeland security team in Alaska.)

The Audrey Eleanor had called Prince Rupert home for ten years prior to us taking her north to Haines, Alaska. Her former owners, Blake and Amy, along with old admirers, showed up for a general inspection. The beer and yarns flow thick and fast. (We had to shovel her out the next day, the B.S. levels were high) It was a great homecoming for the grand old lady after a two year absence. We reluctantly leave our moorage at the Cow Bay docks in Prince Rupert and disappear with muffled engines into drizzle and fog.

As we motored away, little did we know that we had acquired a stow-away who would drive us to the depths of despair. He is darkly hand-some, short and round with glossy black fur and an exceptionally long tail. The little bugger is everywhere. Our rule is that we have enough dry and canned goods aboard to last a month. I have sprout seeds to provide live green stuff. We also experiment with sea asparagus and seaweeds and supplement some of these strange "greens" as the Captain refers to them with fish and crab. Of course, you sometimes come across a little corner store at the end of a falling down dock, which has vegetables lingering in bins that no one else wants. This is why they are still here of course. These tiny supply stores can be miles in between nowhere.

His trail of red lentils gives him away. It's the strangest thing…to see trails of red lentils appearing and disappearing through out the boat. Then beautiful white toilet paper flowers began to show up in the dresser drawers and in closets. These kind of white flowers you sometimes see along the banks of the Yukon River (the toilet paper kind). These ones are the nest type, though.

One of the few things we do not have on board is mice or rat traps. We are three hours out of Prince Rupert and not about to let a little mouse drive us back to port. The Captain reverts back to his days of trapping, and life is exciting. There are water buckets set up with little ramps and string lines strung across the mouths of buckets to rotating bait…none of this is working.

Three days of mouse may not seem like a long time, but we are up close and very personal here…he scratches around at night, and we can hear him under our berth. I start to think that I can hear him breath-ing. He has destroyed a month's worth of beans, rice and a whole extra large bag of lime-flavoured nacho chips has simply vanished. He leaves the empty bag as if to say in your face, people.

When your time comes, your time comes. The Captain gets up early and makes his way to the head (toilet) to find an extremely exhausted mouse swimming laps in the toilet bowl. There is no sympathy; the intruder is immediately pinched by his long tail and lobbed through the air, off the stern of the boat. He hits the water with a plop. The crew and Captain feel a great sense of relief, and a fish receives an early breakfast. We are mouse free!!

The weather has been terrible, so we are now sleeping up in the saloon on the floor. We have better visibility up here. I roll over on the mattress and look down through the focscle to the forward head. You can imagine my horror when I catch a glimpse of a very, very fat furry butt diving into a crevice in the wall. This for sure is Mrs. Mouse and she looks like she will deliver a horde of lentil munchers at any moment.

If we don't catch her before all of those babies are born, we will have to bring Audrey up on the hard and de-mouse her with some nasty chemical-type stuff. My theory about killer chemicals for rodents and bug sprays is, if it kills them, it will kill us. We may be bigger, but it will only take a little longer. To take a 30 tonne yacht up on the hard (land) is extremely expensive. Regardless, there are no facilities in this remote area to handle us. We would have had to live with the mouse infestation for two weeks or more, depending on the weather.

If Mr. Mouse was difficult to catch, Mrs. Mouse makes him look like an amateur. She becomes bold enough to run over us as we try to sleep in the saloon. I have to sleep with my head under the blankets, I am afraid that she will get caught in my hair. The stress of her invasion is driving us crazy. We are doing the sea-going version of Caddyshack. I am beginning to appreciate that we don't have a gun. While I would not miss the mouse, I would be concerned about a hole being blasted in the hull. The Captain has had enough.

She calmly enjoys our peanut butter bait every evening and continues to build toilet paper nests in the hold, in the galley (closer to the peanut butter bait. The stash of toilet paper is almost depleted... things are getting serious. She does not forget however, to leave her lovely little black offerings everywhere that she has been. We are at our wits end.

Necessity IS the mother of invention. Simultaneously we yell, "the heads!" The Captain smears a 2"x 2" piece of blue Styrofoam with the last of the peanut butter. The bait gets set afloat in the head. Well, my goodness gracious if Mrs. Mouse doesn't fall into the same trap as her husband, we find her swimming exhausted in the head the next morning. Without hesitation she is lobbed off the stern of the boat as well, and another fish is fed. If anyone for one second feels any sympathy for this terrorizing critter, you should live with mice in your hice!

P.S. A young Inuit girl that I went to school with in Kugluktuk insisted that if mice was plural for mouse, then hice had to be plural for house, you couldn't have one without the other. People in the house were also a cause for it to be plural. It has stuck in my head. Her English was much better than my Inuktituk.

Cries of the Furies

LOOSE LINES SINK SHIPS

Whales serenade us as we lounge in the natural hot springs of Bishop Bay, near Kitimat, B.C.

…we streak (literally) towards the dock. Waves crash over us and the dock as we scramble and fall trying to reach the Audrey Eleanor.

Grenville Channel, south of Prince Rupert, is deep, dark, long and narrow. Without a north wind, it is well-protected. With the north wind a-blowing, you are in a wind funnel from hell.

Fortunately, there are no winds as we cruise down its narrow depths at the end of October. The fog has rolled in, covering the mountains and spilling over to fill the channels. Audrey's twin Perkin diesel engines rumble in deep rhythm, the muffled sound echoes back off of the steep mountain walls. The fog parts just when we need it to. I am the bow rider, holding onto the short rail with my ears cocked for sounds of other muffled engines. If we come to an abrupt stop, I will flip over the rail and plop into the black water.

We are running with our radar on, but the radar does not see all. Wooden boats often place metal plates on masts or bows as a salute to the scanners that prefer to identify objects made of metal. Radar sometimes misses wooden boats.

Grenville Channel opens up onto Gil Island. We shut the engines down in respect and silently cruise over the face of the ocean where the Queen of the North is laying still and quiet on the bottom of this very cold and black sea. The Audrey Eleanor and crew are so very much smaller than the Queen of the North, a B.C. ferry, that struck Gil Island in March 2006, killing a man and a woman.

The Queen of the North lies on the dark bottom of the ocean floor about 427 meters below us. We feel very insignificant. We have roughly 650 kilometres to travel in this unpredictable month of storms.

The wreck of the Edmund Fitzgerald, a song by Gordon Lightfoot commemorating the ships tragic 1975 sinking in Lake Superior, is playing over and over in my mind. I am praying that the storms of November don't try to out do the storms of October that have battered us since we left Ketchikan, Alaska.

Our radio is giving us grief again. This never happens while we are in a port. We changed our antennae in Ketchikan, but our reception is still sketchy at best.

We swing to portside and motor past Hartley Bay, a Native village that helped to save most of the people off of the Queen of the North. Hartley Bay responded to the distress call on March 21, just before midnight. The Queen of the North took about an hour to sink and the actual time is debated as 12:25 a.m. or 12:43 a.m. on March 22, 2006. Fishermen with small fishing boats and people with recreational boats braved the black night and howling winds of up to seventy five kilometres per hours to save the people that were on the ferry.

Hartley Bay is a picturesque village with a wild mountain backdrop that reminds me of the villages on the Mackenzie River, N.W.T., that I grew up in. (see The White Girl Series)

A twin Otter glides in behind us for a water landing in front of the village. The Captain now swings us to starboard and we head up Douglas Channel toward Bishop Bay Hot Springs.

It's a sign. Streaks of sunshine suddenly break through the cloud cover and the shattered rays feel like Sunday morning in a mountainous cathedral. God rays I call them; we have not seen the sun in weeks.

Thank you Goddess, we are involved in divine intervention on the top deck, steering Audrey from the flying bridge. Warmth from the sun penetrates wet clothes; we steam a bit as we pass beneath unbelievable double rainbows. Spirits are carried upward with the steam, wrapped in smiles of thankfulness

Bishop Bay comes into view. The tide is high so it takes a few minutes for the little house at the springs to come into sight. Whales are spouting and singing all around us. The sea is flat calm. This is magic, this is heaven on earth and we cannot believe what we are experiencing, all of this just a few miles from Kitimat, B.C.

A fifteen foot fishing boat is tied to the small dock. The radio onboard the fishing boat is barking but there is no sign of the Captain or crew. Bishop Bay Hot Springs is a five-minute jaunt from the dock where we have secured our ship. We have walked down to the raised camping area and made lots of noise, hoping to rouse the crew of the empty fish boat. No one responds, no one is in sight.

While we look forward to new conversation, the plan is to spend the afternoon bare-naked in the hot springs with a bottle of cold white wine being serenaded by the sirens of the deep, the grey whales. Where is that crew??

Thoughts of a hot bath overcome modesty; we strip down and creep into the hot water inside the hut. We have a full-sized shower onboard the Audrey Eleanor, and, while the 25-gallon hot water tank makes sure you leave clean, there is nothing left over for luxury. And let's face it, there is nothing that can replace being fully submerged in clean, hot water. Moist heat penetrates damp, cold bodies and feels so very good.

A concrete hut houses the main body of the hot springs. It is built over the pool and encompasses a natural rock. A rope is suspended from the ceiling, which enables you to swing through the pool. Past crews have left their mark by registering the names of M.V.s (motor vessels) and sailboats on the concrete walls.

My wine glass sits in one of the window slits. Narrow cuts in the hut allow for limited peeps into the outside world. Through the steam from the hot springs we see that a steady rain has begun. Suddenly, torrential rain begins to pound on the tin roof; this is rather romantic as we settle deeper into the beautiful hot water, sipping the very good white wine, in real glasses, no less.

Something has changed, this is not so romantic anymore; the wind has come up. A peek through the small windows reveals a sideways rain en-route and presenting itself as a solid wall of black. The empty fishing boat has vanished. With winds coming up fiercely, the waves are being thrown over the top of the dock and slamming hard on the beam of the Audrey Eleanor.

We streak (literally) toward the dock trying to pull on soggy clothes while we slip and slide naked in cold muck. A ramp that accesses the dock is twisting sideways and threatening to dislocate itself from the main body of the dock. Waves are crashing over the dock, and drenching us as we try to physically reach out and grab the Audrey Eleanor.

Remember the rays of sunshine and calm waters that we arrived on? Well, we had tied our ship accordingly. All of our lines had been tied too loosely they are now stretched taut in the wind and have put Audrey totally out of our reach, allowing no access.

Trying to pull a 30 tonne wooden yacht broadside to the wind is mostly impossible. We hang on to the lines waiting for a lull in the storm to get close enough so one of us can jump aboard. Someone has to be aboard our precious ship if this dock decides to leave with her still attached.

Waves are staccato, shot-gunning burst of grey seawater through the cracks in the dock. This is serious; the dock is separating from the ramp. Enough, the Captain decides to walk the line like a tightrope walker and jumps the last few feet to land on the bow. How does he do shit like that? I am glad that he is the one aboard; he deals with the engines way better than I do.

Of course, the wind dies down once he has secured the ship. Someone flips the switch, the light comes back on, God rays split the clouds and fog once again in their brilliance. Whales assume their songs with a deep resonation that vibrates mountains, boat hulls and bones. Echoes off the deep green peaks give us whale celebration in stereo.

Soaking wet, mud splattered and mostly naked, we look at each other and laugh. Lots of a bottle of wine still sits back in the hut at the hot springs, we can jump back into the hot water to wash our clothes and ourselves.

We settle back in the open area in front of the hut, we now know that we have the bay to ourselves. Dusk paints a pale pink sky that slowly climbs over the silver grey of the clouds. A spout of water blown high into the air by a whale breaks the solitude. They grow quiet with the approach of night in this wondrous place that man has not managed to decimate.

P.S. For a week, the Canadian Coast Guard has been calling "Sécurité" on the radio, searching for a missing person. We did not talk to the crew on the fish boat, which was registered out of Vancouver. People in isolated places tend to be very friendly; your life can depend on it. The village of Hartley Bay demonstrated this when they rescued the passengers off of the Queen of the North. The Captain of the fishing boat was not feeling very social; we wondered if this was the boat that the Coast Guard was looking for. Join us soon for another ADVENTURE OF THE AUDREY ELEANOR.

Cries of the Furies

MILBANKE SOUND

We spend an uneasy night tucked slightly behind Arthur Island in Mathieson Channel. The hook is dropped, our only barricade from a sou'easter is a small log boom. There has been no defining wind direction for the past few weeks; just a continual blow with ratings from storm to small vessel warnings on the weather channel. Other than my fears of a blow up, the night has been uneventful. The anchor is pulled and we look forward to an easy cruise into Shearwater, which is beside Bella Bella, on the Inside Passage of B.C., Canada. A small chop on the sea is riffles from the local breeze, and nothing more. If there were swells, it

Captain Rick Cousins cleans a grey cod on the swimming grid (most of this grid gets ripped off on the rocks in the next story, "Ivory Island") of the Audrey Eleanor. The calm before the storm, dinner will soon be served up fresh from the sea.

would indicate that there are big seas brewing further out.

Audrey is coming into view of Lady Douglas Island when we notice flashing lights in the sky in front of us. Very unusual...the Captain, who once flew his own plane, is excited that this Beaver is coming in so close to say good morning. I am the cautious one, this Beaver is just slightly above our masthead light and he is flashing his landing lights and anything else that he can light up to catch our attention.

A slight dip of the wings means hello to me. This pilot is going out of his way to get his message across. His engines roar over the saloon, he continues to wag his wings and flash his landing gear. He quickly gains altitude and disappears towards the north. I say to the Captain that I believe we have just received a warning. The Captain reminds me that we are very protected in Mathieson Channel. Our only exposure to the open ocean will be when we round Lady Douglas Island. There are only a very few miles until we can tuck into Reid Channel, it will be a piece of cake. I feel better...how bad can it be?

It's a relatively narrow channel between Lady Douglas and Lake Islands; lots of small, hazardous rocks and islands narrow the passage down even further. There is no quick turn-around space. Audrey is 54 feet in length with a 13 foot beam (width) at her widest point; she is cigar-shaped. With her displacement hull, she cuts through the waves rather than rides them, having a narrow beam means that she doesn't respond well to being hit broadside by rough seas. In other words, if we have to take it on the beam, she could broach or fall on her side into the trough of the sea. I really don't like when this happens; it truly makes your heart stop.

We've come between Lady Douglas and Lake Islands; Cecilia Island is not far off our port side. Squeezing between Lake Island and a large rock to our starboard side, we now know why the plane was trying to warn us. This is a very shallow area, which causes the waves to basically bounce back off of the ocean floor and creates standing waves. We are in them, they are 14 feet high...WE CANNOT TURN AROUND!

These monsters are threatening to roll us up on the rocks. The Captain's only alternative is to take us out to sea. We have to take these waves head on, so as to avoid any sideways contact that will roll us side over side until we smash on the reef. We head out into the open ocean, the waves are building; they are huge. Chairs that we use at the chart table are rolling on the floor and smashing against the walls. Books are falling from the shelves, cupboard doors are slamming back and forth and cans and pots are colliding, creating a terrible noise. My plants and window herb garden have fallen and smashed on the floor.

I am hanging onto a small piece of wood trim that runs along the dash with my fingertips and trying to wedge myself against the chart table so that I don't end up on the floor rolling around with the chairs.

My head is hanging down below the dash, and I am praying quietly, this is terror beyond anything that I ever want to do again. The huge waves are smashing against the hull and Audrey shudders with the impact. Her ribs are being battered as she fights the seas and we can hear her moan with the effort of staying afloat. I raise my head just as I hear the Captain yell, "Holy..."

I have known this man for 32 years, and this is the first time that I've ever seen him afraid. I know for sure we won't make it.

A giant wave smashes directly against the almost sixty year old front window; it cannot withstand that kind of impact again. Once the window smashes out, it will only take a few minutes for us to start to take on water. The cold black sea will rush in and swamp us.

The Captain looks at me for a moment.

"I have to try something that I've never done before," he yells. "Hang on!"

A huge wave slams into the bow; the water is thrown way up and over the flying bridge. Fifty four feet of boat are racing skyward, she's dancing on her stern and then we plummet down into the trough. Upward again, with water crashing outside the view from the window, speeding downward toward the sea bed, we are a submarine.

I hear the Captain counting, "One, two, three..." I understand. Generally the seventh wave is the biggest, he is looking for the biggest wave! When we top the wave, he will try to turn us on the crest before we slide into the trough again. If he doesn't make it, we will be hit broadside and we will be lost forever. The Audrey Eleanor and crew will be rolled over and over, ground and pummelled into the bottom of this merciless ocean.

We crest a huge wave, and manage a quick look between us. You hope you've been able to convey the things that you should have said to each other, plus goodbye, in that split second. There may never be a chance to say the unsaid, this could be our final moments on earth. The time has come and gone to say what needs saying, the Captain yells, "Hang on!"

He throws one engine in forward and one in reverse, pours the diesel to the engines and we begin to pivot on the top of a giant wave. In slow motion, she begins her turn. The bow is heading downward and we charge back down into the trough. Sound has been sucked out of the air, it feels like we are in a vacuum.

We are heading back toward land on a following sea. Remember what I said about these waters being really shallow? Audrey is now fighting to climb a mountain of water in front of her and the surge bearing down from behind is threatening to break onto our stern deck and crush us. We are worried that we will bottom out in the trough.

I stand on the back deck watching as our grand lady fights to climb this wall of ocean. The mountain of water is 20 feet high. Her engines are pounding like double heartbeats; the props churn in the wave. Twin props scream as the wall of water lifts and exposes them. She fights, she screams and struggles to lift us up to the crest of the next wave. She does it. She does it! She carries us forward...we truly have made it. The Captain surfs us toward land, safety, and Reid Channel.

It is only 9 a.m. What a morning! This adventure happened before our morning coffee. Reid Channel is narrow, protected, and the waters are calm. It is impossible to believe that minutes ago we were fighting for our lives.

Now, we are slowly cruising into this beautiful marine park. There are books mixed in with the dirt and broken plants that validate that we actually just smashed our way through mountains of water.

We had thought to check out Oliver Cove on our way by; the diving is supposed to be great, but it is still early in the day. The thought of a little socializing and fresh food in Shearwater is drawing us out into the open sea again. We will have to stick our noses out past Ivory Island and into Seaforth Channel, but what the heck; a person can only have one really horrific experience on the ocean in one-day right?? Besides as the Captain likes to say, "God hates a coward!"

This story will be continued in the next Adventure of The Audrey Eleanor, "Ivory Island".

Cries of the Furies

IVORY ISLAND

The saloon onboard the Audrey Eleanor, looking through into the galley. Captain Rick Cousins and First Mate Dawn Kostelnik fall to the floor in exhaustion.

In the previous adventure, the Audrey Eleanor and crew took a beating while trying to creep undetected past the Furies and Mother Nature into Milbanke Sound and through Reid Channel. We managed to escape after 20 foot seas threatened to roll us side over side and dredge us into the ocean floor.

It is surreal cruising down Reid Channel in calm waters after being battered minutes earlier by huge waves. I have to pinch myself to make sure that I am still alive. It is one of those moments where you wonder if you haven't actually crossed over into another world or dimension and someone should show up soon to give you directions on how to proceed.

The directions come... from the helm. The Captain decides that we should cruise into Oliver Cove to check out possible anchorage and make the big decision, do we go or do we stay? It is nine o'clock in the morning and Shearwater is only a few hours away. We have been living off of dry goods, mostly what the mice have left of the lentils (the undamaged bags...I know what you are thinking!!) and whatever the Captain manages to bring up in the crab traps or catch on a hook...you can actually get sick of crab, you know.

What are the odds of experiencing another extreme adventure the same morning after our experience at Milbanke Sound? We have studied the charts. The direction of the waves we have just come through could make it rough going at the tip of Ivory Island. It should only be for a short distance; the tide has turned and could help ease the ride. God hates a coward. We're going for it!

Between Cecilia Island, Ivory Island and the Don Peninsula, there is a minefield of rocks. Coming out of Reid Channel, you have a very narrow passage, with Ivory Island to your starboard side. The lighthouse on Ivory Island then works as your navigational aid to direct you safely up Seaforth Channel. Most of the rocks in this area are "just" submerged, waves smashing over and on them. Verify what the charts say; this is an extremely dangerous area...stay on the road.

The Captain edges Audrey out into the channel...so far so good. Swells begin to rise, and the wind picks up as we head out. The beginnings of waves on top of the swells are making me nervous. The swell/wave action is increasing; a combination of the seas building and the waves are beginning to break over the bow again. My hands begin to shake and I'm having difficulty hanging on to my little ledge on the windowsill. Ivory Island is close, just off to starboard... the waves are beginning to resemble the monsters that we have just escaped.

Why on earth would we do this again on purpose? Here we go again. I have lost the feeling in both of my arms and they are jumping around like some invisible puppet master has control of them and just wants me to look foolish. Thank the Goddess, the Captain decides that this is enough for one day, makes the turn and is taking us back toward Reid Channel.

A white curtain drops in front of us. An inversion of cold air hitting warmer water or vice versa; we are in a fog bank. The inversion has also instantly steamed up all of our windows. They are running with condensation and it's impossible to see out. Amazingly, as soon as we are out of the huge waves, my arms become my own again. Physiological, you think? You bet. I am terrified!

I have a squeegee; I am running from window to window clearing off the moisture so that the Captain has some visibility in this rock mine-field. The mouth of Reid Channel is very narrow and hard to distinguish in fair weather; the fog and rain are making it impossible. Cecilia Island looms out of the fog in front of us.

We nose toward the shore, trying to get our position. Something doesn't feel right. I run to the stern of the boat and look outside. We are churning up mud!!

I run, yelling, toward the saloon. The Captain has already figured that we have a problem and has thrown Audrey into reverse. The wake of the boat lifts us up and back out. He switches to neutral. The fog has cleared enough; we can see our bow is not in Reid Channel. Our nose is stuck into a little bight (indent) on Cecilia Island...but where on Cecilia Island?! Are we either too far to the east or to the west of the channel? The fog swirling around us is thick, too thick for us to see anything in the distance.

A sudden rush of fresh wind tosses us and drives the fog further out/ This we don't want to see. All around us the waves are smashing on barely submerged rocks, it looks like those pictures you see of the Oregon coast during a storm, I'd always thought that the waves crashing on the rocks with spray flying high into the air looked wild and beautiful. Up close, it's wild and bloody dangerous. There is no way out, I tell you!

The Captain is struggling to maintain our position; waves are making it difficult to hold a steady course. Our bow is in the bight and our stern is positioned between two huge, submerged rocks. They look to be about three feet below the surface, with the one on our portside breaking free of the ocean now and again. Our draft is 4'6". Those rocks will gouge and crack the hull apart.

A decision is made; we are in reverse and heading to starboard to find the channel. The Captain has us turned slightly to the right and he is waiting, waiting again for that bigger wave. The wave comes, lifts us up and carries us over the rock; I can hear ripping and tearing and run back to the stern. Our tender is strapped to the transom, and below it is what's left of the swim grid. The rock that was only partly submerged has ripped off two feet of the swim grid and a section of chrome from the side, we are that close. We have only our eyes and the Captain's instincts to guide us through this mess. There is no channel.

The waves toss salt water 10 feet into the air; these are the easy ones to see and to avoid. The deadly ones are the deep, dark swirls. Are they real, or illusion? After trying to look into and through water, your mind starts to play tricks on you. Was that another rock or simply a shadow of the depths??

To portside, the mouth of Reid Channel comes into view; we have done it, again. God protects drunks, fools and little children; we fit all these categories, depending on the day.

To this day, I don't know how the Captain brought us through those rocks. If you ever get a chance, check out Canadian chart 3710 and you will understand. Losing part of the swim grid and that little piece of chrome was so minimal in comparison to what could have happened. It is an unbelievable feat, and an incredible ability to read water by the Captain once again, in the same day and almost in the same hour, saved our lives!

Again, we are safely in Reid Channel and heading for Oliver Cove. Audrey cruises into the cove and the anchor is dropped. It is 11 o'clock in the morning; we both fall on the saloon floor, exhausted. The last thing that I remember is looking through the window and watching the trees swinging quickly by; we are truly swinging on the hook. We sleep on the floor, like the dead we could have been, for hours. Finally the cold creeps up and in from the hold, sneaking into our bodies.

The Captain lights our Dickinson stove in the galley; the temperature is dropping. From our snug anchorage we can see out into Reid Channel. The wind is managing to drop down over the tree tops, causing us to swing like a huge pendulum. You could get quite dizzy from the motion if you don't concentrate on something other than the inside movement.

For three days we wait out the weather in the Cove. There is no traffic in Reid Channel until the afternoon of the third day. Waves in the channel have built to four feet, so when we see a troller heading south in the channel, it is hard to read the size of her. The back deck is blocked from sight by the waves. The Captain hails the troller on the radio, "Little white fishing boat, little white fishing boat come in please."

Our radio, per usual, is not working properly; the Captain tries the call again and again. A more persistent call goes out, "Lttle white fishing boat in Reid Channel, across from Oliver Cove come in PLEASE!"

The reply finally comes back, in heavily Portuguese-accented English, "Me-e-ester, she's thirty two feet long!"

Profuse apologies from the Captain are followed by a request for weather and sea conditions once the Portuguese boat reaches the lighthouse at Ivory Island. Sure enough, 30 minutes later, there is static on our radio. Nothing that we can decipher, but a well-intentioned reply nonetheless.

More traffic appears. It's a tug this time, heading north. They have just come from where we want to go, perfect. After a request for sea conditions from the Captain, the tug Captain comes back with questions.

"How big is your boat? What is your power? Well, considering your size and power you had better run for it, it won't get any better in this area until spring."

I lose the feeling in my arms again, navigating the bumpy and nerve-wracking Seaforth Channel, but we make it to safe harbour at Shearwater.

P.S. This was a major storm with no boats running for three days, not even the tugs and those guys move in almost anything. The B.C. ferry spent three days hiding behind or beside Princess Royal Island. I bet everyone onboard became great friends. Follow the North Star concludes this string of three stories, with more great adventures on the other side, come join us aboard the Audrey Eleanor.

Cries of the Furies

FOLLOW THE NORTH STAR

...she attempted to tie herself to a wall in the rolling galley.

Rain and fog, rain and fog. A soggy Captain heads out to check crab traps early in the morning before the winds come up to rage and blow the channel clear.

The thought of leaving Shearwater by sea is too traumatic. If I am jumping ship, this is my last chance to do so.

Shearwater is located on Denny Island, across the water from Bella Bella, a Native seaside community located on the coast of B.C., Canada. My escape vehicle could be B.C. Ferries, which makes a scheduled stop at Bella Bella. Or, I could jump into a small floatplane and fly into Port Hardy on Vancouver Island. I would be safe and have to live with the fact that I deserted my ship and my Captain. I am still considering it.

An eighty foot tug registered out of Juneau, Alaska, has been our phantom companion since we left Prince Rupert more than a week ago.

As they vaporize in the fog, so do our communications with them on our none-too-stable radio. They are a ghost ship that offers the small condolence of, "Someone else is out here."

With the surge of storms, we have seen little life moving on the raging seas. Tucking into Oliver Cove, we wait for our chance to make a break into Seaforth Channel and run for Shearwater and civilization.

B.C. Ferries have quit running and the tugs are hiding out with their bows stuck in bights; the storms of November are early. Days later, we made the break for Shearwater.

The big Juneau tug follows us into Shearwater. Waiting at the payphone for a chance to call my kids before we take on our next big crossing, Queen Charlotte Straight, I notice the tugboat Captain's wife is ahead of me; there is little privacy in the area surrounding the payphone.

It is wrenches my heart, listening to her talking to children and grandchildren in the southern U.S. Trying to keep tears under control she bids them a final farewell. She is certain that once back onboard the tug, she is motoring toward to her death. Crying softly, she hangs up the phone and attempts to quiet her sobs; she passes me with head hung low. Such bravery in such a diminutive woman. Would you climb on board a vessel that you were positive was carrying you to your grave? My mind is reeling, how often does that float plane leave for the outside world?

During their previous crossing of Queen Charlotte Sound, the Juneau tug struggled with gigantic waves cresting on top of 20-foot swells. The Captain's wife attempted to tie herself to the wall in the galley to prevent battery of herself within that confined and dangerous area. A rogue wave presented itself on already colossal rollers and nailed them directly on the beam. The impact caused the commercial-sized fridge/freezer to slam to the floor and wedge up against the door. Her access to the outside world was cut off until a crew member thought to look for her.

She was beaten around in the galley for four hours before any of the crew could leave their posts to rescue her. No windows and no escape; she was in her coffin on a roller coaster ride in the black. When the tug arrived at Campbell River, she was treated for minor injuries and major physiological trauma. She is about to face her demons again, in this winter of storms.

What I had not realized was that this crossing of Queen Charlotte Straight was Captain Rick's nemesis as well. We had survived Dixon Entrance and were alive, if badly shaken, after the threat of being ground into the rocky bottom of a shallow sea in Milbanke Sound. And, how about grabbing a wave that lifted us over ragged rocks by Ivory Island? Wasn't that enough, haven't the dues been paid? There is no mercy in the sea, no such thing as having paid enough dues.

I had lost feeling in my arms after the terrifying encounter with Milbanke Sound; this leaves me with another concern. This is the point that I refuse to get back on the boat.

I am the only crew; it's the two of us against this literal craziness. My arms are working again, but I am afraid that I could possibly have a stroke or a heart attack if we get pummeled again. The Captain is an amazing guy. If I did have any of the above, he would have to deal with three temperamental ladies: me, Mother Nature and Audrey Eleanor. I know that if I am having a heart attack or stroke it isn't because it is a calm sunny day. Even he is not that good. My concern is that I could end up being more trouble than is worth the risk.

Coming up Seaforth Channel, my hands had been shaking so uncontrollably that I cannot hold on to anything to stabilize myself. I suggest that he call one of the boys and and asks them come to replace me as the crew.

There is wisdom in drinking too much beer. Shearwater is having its Halloween party this night. The Captain insists that we go ashore, this would be a great opportunity to relax, engage in conversation with people other than ourselves, and swill beer.

Such a great time! People here are glad to have someone new to talk to as well. The night carries on into the dawn. Everyone is swept up in an alcoholic haze; we will be best friends forever and all of that wonderful stuff.

The next morning, I am praying for a swift death. That man has his moments, he knows I get sick as a dog and hope for death after a night of great social activity…I am back on board the Audrey Eleanor, listing in my bunk with a major hangover and en-route to Queen Charlotte Sound.

This is the time to take on the Sound and the Straight. I watch the moons, the barometer, hold my mouth just right and sniff the salty breeze.

I will walk on water to avoid crossing a Straight or a sound at tide change, not at slack but at the change. I believe that if there is an opportunity for a rough crossing, this is when it will happen.

Our famous crossing of Dixon Entrance sickens me to this day. At this moment, if I think about that crossing and close my eyes, I am falling out of the saloon door and into the trough of the wild seas. There are times when you have no choice in the matter, but the tides are in our favour for the next two days.

In order to time our crossing perfectly, we are anchoring at Hecate Island tonight and then running for the safety of Vancouver Island early tomorrow morning. Goldstream Harbour on Hecate Island is our destination. It is a difficult passage to distinguish and tricky to navigate. With a narrow and rock-strewn entrance to the inside, we swing up and in on the crest of a building sea.

An 80 pound hook is dropped, and we settle in for the night. A full moon strikes a mirrored path on the calm waters of the harbour. The stars, I can tickle their bellies. Standing on the flying bridge, I hear the thunder of monster waves crashing against the small natural breakwater which creates this bay. White froth and foam of cresting waves shimmer and are accentuated in the full moon; tons of water smash against the little wall yet again. I am feeling very unsure that this damned big ocean is going to stay on its own side of the island.

Huge rocks, crowned with old growth trees, stunted and malformed, assure me that they have managed to hang on by twisted and gnarled roots for decades. I look back at the surreal calm in the anchorage and there in all of its solitary glory sparkles the reflection of the Big Dipper with the gleam of the North Star. None of the other stars are apparent to me, but in crystal clear view is the Big Dipper. I am thinking, this is a sign, we need to turn around and run as fast as we can to the Yukon. We should not do this crossing.

The first pale, pink light creeps across Goldstream Harbour as we prepare to weigh anchor. I hand crank the 80 pound anchor and 200 feet of rope and chain that make up our rode. I cannot haul the anchor up past the 40-foot mark, this is our water depth. The anchor is sitting on the bottom refusing to leave. I finally yell at the Captain that if he thinks that he can do better, he should.

When the Captain manages to pull the anchor free of the seabed, we see that a huge boulder has lodged itself on the anchor flutes. My active mind is whirling, another sign, my god we need to turn back. I don't want to do this crossing. Yeah, well, "God hates a coward," and we leave our little haven and turn to starboard.

"Sécurité, sécurité" breaks up on the radio weather channel...we know this chant by heart. Swells are beginning to build as we nose our bow out into Queen Charlotte Straight and beyond Cape Caution. We now have to run as far and as fast as our eight knots per hour will carry us toward God's Pocket. There is no turning back.

Swells are building and carrying us towards Vancouver Island. Audrey climbs the walls of water, we coast 12 feet down into the trough and up we go again. Very pleasant, if only I could relax and enjoy it. A black line on the horizon signifies that a storm is moving in; God, let us be off of the wide-open ocean by then. Up we go and down we glide, we are on a gigantic powered surfboard. I can see Vancouver Island! This is the warm and gentle south; this is where we want to spend the winter aboard the Audrey Eleanor. This is safety. It doesn't matter that nirvana is still miles away, having the visual, no matter how deceptive the concept of safety is, is wonderful.

Up and down, up and down, closer and closer we get. We are at God's Pocket (fantastic diving) and the seas are such that we are going to continue on to Port Hardy. There is nothing physically wrong with my heart when Mother Nature is not terrorizing me. We are almost there!

P.S. We never saw the tug from Juneau, Alaska, again. Knowing their cruising speed and with the size of the waves that we watched from the security of Goldstream Harbour, I can only assume that they had another extreme crossing of Queen Charlotte Straight. Once the Captain's wife gets to her home in the southern part of the U.S., I truly wish that she never has to make that crossing again. This story is for Willie Olson. Join us again for another ADVENTURE OF THE AUDREY ELEANOR.

Cries of the Furies

THE SCREAMS OF THE FURIES

The Captain is asleep with his good hearing ear in the pillow…I can feel the weight of it as it as it gets closer, roaring like an old White Pass steam engine, determined to run us down. The Audrey Eleanor is pulsating with the sound…

The Audrey Eleanor, in the calm after the storm.

It has been a handful of years since the magnificent, giant, old-growth cedars of Stanley Park in Vancouver, Canada, were flattened to the earth. Hurricane winds ripped and tore their roots from the very land that sustained them. As they thundered to the earth, causing humankind to tremble, we were at the anchor on an old wooden boat.

Fifty four feet and thirty tonnes of old wooden yacht must be held off of jagged rocks by a chain and a cast iron Danforth anchor in hurricane -force winds. Our anchor had been set earlier in the afternoon and should be stuck in the mud. We hope so.

The Audrey Eleanor, a 1948 custom wooden yacht, is anchored in Potts Lagoon, located at the northern end of Vancouver Island. We had slipped away from our berth at the government dock on Malcolm Island, disappearing into the fog like a shadowy ghost ship. After days of pouring rain and windstorms, we are making our weather break from Sointula on Malcolm Island.

Our quest is to find a safe and semi-permanent harbour on a more southern portion of Vancouver Island. It is early morning, and we are soon enveloped in a grizzly gray drizzle.

Steel-coloured ocean leaves no definition, no distinction against steely skies. Flat silver water appears oily. We motor off into nothingness, I wonder if we will drop off the end of the world? There is no indication that a storm is brewing as we search for the slicing dorsal fins of killer whales. A family pod has been sighted recently here and we are on high alert. This is an area of rubbing beaches for the giant "wolves of the sea".

A change in tide swings us slightly to one side. H-m-m-m...is it tidal currents or are the waves coming up? A Seaspan tug is starboard to us; he is making a run to catch the slack tide at Seymour Narrows. Spray from the sea is beginning to break over his bow.

"She's coming up," states the Captain. "We are going to look for shelter before it gets dark."

We have no radio contact. In Ketchikan, Alaska, we replaced the antennae. In Port Hardy, B.C., we replaced the radio. Our reward for this costly process is a static squawk.

Whomp, whomp, whomp, the Canadian Coast Guard is hovering overhead in a very large helicopter. It's nice to know that they are there, but we don't want to give them a reason to stick around. Audrey's bow points us toward our destination, Potts Lagoon on Cracroft Island. The search and rescue helicopter swings off to the starboard side and disappears from sight. The anchor is to be set in the mud.

Our new neighbourhood is made up of several float houses. This may be a summer camp, we are not sure. The lagoon is not very large, with signs of an old wharf at one end. It has a beach type that indicates it is good crabbing territory. There is still enough light to drop a few crab pots. Gray skies darken slowly into black. I feel that someone is watching us from the float houses. The hair stands up on the back of my neck, I don't like this sense of being ogled while sitting out in the blackening middle of nowhere. We circle the float house, intending to be neighborly. No one responds to our hellos.

Hurricane-force winds begin as a distant rumble, sounding very much like the old White Pass train roaring down the tracks into the city of Whitehorse, Yukon. I can feel the weight of it in my sleep. Closer and closer it comes. I sit upright with a start, wanting to stop this bad dream. It continues, the weight is a heavy pressure in my inner ear; it pulses like a migraine in my temples. This is no dream; it's a Goddamned nightmare! An entity has arrived and is attempting to bulldoze us over! The Furies are coming, The Furies are coming!

Audrey Eleanor is pulsating with the sound. My Captain is asleep in the saloon with his good hearing ear in the pillow. I sleep with the hard of hearing Captain, drop the anchor when need be and I do the dishes, damn it! I am the crew. Captain Rick must be dreaming that his perfect Perkins diesels are vibrating us toward the Mexican border; regardless it is time to share this experience with him.

I waken him to the all-engulfing screams of the Furies. A hundred shrieking banshees are blasting us in their rage. A wall of wind hits the Audrey Eleanor with mighty force. Icy fingers of wind become steel. They rip and tear at the canvas. Swung hard to starboard, the chain attached to the anchor stretches taut and jerks us hard about. We stumble and fall with the motion.

Monsoon rains pummel the saloon roof. Blasting rain resonates on above us. I feel that I am inside a tin can that is being pelted with small rocks, the noise is deafening. The Captain yells for the spotlight as he flashes into action, setting radar and depth sounders on high alert. Wrestling the saloon door open, he shines the spotlight into the harbour. The light stops dead, a solid black wall of water greets him, we see nothing.

No visibility, coupled with the deafening rain, means we have no way of knowing whether we are dragging our anchor over the floor of the ocean. There is no sight; there is no sound except for the pelting rain.

The alarm on the radar is set to go off if we get within 50 feet of a solid obstacle, but that would be too late. If we are blown up on the rocks in this blackest of nights, it could cost us our lives.

Our radar is particular as to what it will reveal. I jump up to check the depth sounder repeatedly. We are maintaining a water level of 45 feet beneath our hull and it is low tide. As the tide rises, so will we. So far so good, but there will be no sleep this night.

I get a whiff of wood smoke. My God! Now what, we are on a wooden boat, are we on a wooden boat that is on fire? Huge tanks of diesel contained in our hull would set up a blaze for all the world to see.

A frantic survey reveals that we are not about to be cremated. For sure, someone is living on the float houses and doesn't want to be seen. The fury of the night compels them to light a fire or freeze. Our silent neighbour has started a wood fire in one of the float houses. I knew I could feel eyes on us. This is creepy. I want to go home.

In true Yukon tradition, we settle into a long night of cribbage. Yelling at each other at the top of our lungs, we attempt to outlast the storm, 15/4, 15/6…and listening for things that go "bump" in the night under the Audrey Eleanor.

P.S. Later, we found the force of the jerk on the chain to the anchor caused the cast iron stanchion to bend. You can see it still, should you decide to visit. And so, the journey begins. Join us soon for another ADVENTURE OF THE AUDREY ELEANOR.

Cries of the Furies

GARDEN OF EDEN

One of many "Garden of Edens" we encountered on our adventures, pictured below, is Petersburg, Alaska, a fishing and logging village that has purposely refused cruise ships to commercialize their lives. They maintain their identity and have a healthy and sustainable economy. Their children will be able to fish unpolluted waters and breathe clean air.

Hurricane-force winds mean it's just another day on the west coast. We have weathered two such storms in Potts Lagoon, located towards the north end of Vancouver Island. These are the winds that flattened Stanley Park in Vancouver, B.C., Canada. Four days of sitting in the rain is wearing on us. The crab traps are providing fresh "meat", but new sights and people that we have yet to meet are just around the corner…. time is dragging.

We were anchored beside a summer floating camp in Potts Lagoon, three houses set on floats, which looked to be a great place to hide out during the summer. It appears that someone had this idea as well, but are hiding out for the winter. The first night that we were slammed by the hurricane winds, we could smell wood smoke. We distinctly smelled wood smoke as the storm raged around us. This is not a good thing on a wooden boat, and it becomes terrifying in the black of the night with the wild winds of the Furies screaming at you.

We set out in the zodiac to see if we could raise anyone in the float houses. We circle the houses, called hello several times, with no response. Whoever is inside does not want to socialize, we understand. Every night we smell the wood smoke, our anonymous neighbours don't use any lights and we never see them. After four days of knowing that you have someone living beside you that doesn't want to be seen, well, it just wears you out. I want to go, these anonymous neighbours are giving me the creeps.

Today's the day! We are attempting to make it to Port Neville. Audrey heads up Knight Inlet and cruises around Minstrel Island. It's bumpy, but we moving. As we get closer to Johnstone Straight, the seas start to build again. The Coast Guard out of Comox are following us in a helicopter (they have done this before, it is getting personal). It's rough going, but compared to some of the rides we've had, it's bearable. Maybe it's the hovering help above us that makes the rough seas easier to take. Nope, the waves build and we are forced to duck into Burial Cove.

The anchor is dropped and we wait for the tide to turn. Anchored beside us in the cove is a one hundred and twenty-foot ship that has been re-constructed and is now used as a floating bunkhouse, possibly for a logging crew. The crews must be on leave in Campbell River. It's pretty quiet on board from what we can see and can't hear.

It's high slack tide and we are running for Port Neville before the tide starts to turn. We will duck into the government wharf, which has a reputation as being a rough place to dock with the swirling currents and tides

The Coast Guard is back above us as we near Seymour Narrows. There is a barge in front of us. We debate about getting up close and letting it break the waves for us. Time is against us, we will have to fight our own battle with the wind and waves. We are only a few kilometres from the dock and the barge is on the other side of the Straight. We wonder who the Coast Guard is looking for. We have not talked to family and friends in days; we hope it isn't us they search for.

The dock is to our portside. It has huge big beams and it looks very well made. The current is swirling around the piles; this is going to be an exciting moorage. I am on the bow trying to either lasso the piles or jump for it. Sometimes being five feet tall is limiting. The current is determined to take us back out into the channel.

I can hear a voice…. no it's not the Coast Guard or God either. There is a petite lady standing on the dock yelling at me to throw her the rope. Thank you Goddess, the rope is thrown and she secures the bow. The Captain brings in her stern and we are home free.

Lorna introduces herself as the second-generation homesteader, mail lady, entrepreneur, and keeper of the government docks. She is appreciated.

She invites us to come ashore to see her family's homestead and also throws in an invitation for dinner. The sun is starting to set as we head up the gangway. An old two-storey building sits at the head of the dock walkway, we stroll towards it. The sun is just setting as we reach land… maybe we did drown out there. This has to be heaven, or at the very least, this is the Garden of Eden.

The Captain and I both stand with mouths wide open in awe. We are at the gateway to her property. There are green rolling hills with lush emerald grass that's been recently cut (this is November). Off to the right. at the top of a green knoll, is the most perfect little log cabin; lights twinkle in the lace-lined windows. Several apple trees are scattered throughout the acreage that still have red apples clinging to their branches.

Underneath the apple trees are deer, small ones and big ones, no shy ones. As they notice us, they come over to visit. Lorna states, "They are looking for apples."

She hands us a few apples that she has hidden in her pockets. The deer walk right up to us and nuzzle our sides looking for their supper. Apparently, they will follow a person around all day begging for apples. This year's fawn looks up with big, soft brown eyes; you know that you have to find just one more apple, somewhere.

The two-storey building is the old homestead that Lorna grew up in. Rough, hand-hewn timbers are silver with age; it is now an art shop for tourists in the summer. Her new home, which is the post office as well, sits just beyond the homestead. We amble towards her house with our deer entourage bumping at our hands and hips. They have become a nuisance and a pain, funny how quickly that can happen!

Lorna lives here by herself. The log cabin is uninhabited; I wasn't sure why the lights were on, maybe it makes her feel like she has neighbours. She has a generator for power and keeps her marine radio on to listen to passing ships. Bears are curious about the noise that the generator creates, or maybe it is simply the shortest route to the apples. She has bumped noses with the bears often.

We tell Lorna that our radio has been giving us grief forever, she proceeds to give us a brief but thorough lesson in marine radios. Sécurité, sécurité, sécurité...doesn't that mean GOOD MORNING?? We have spent most of our cruising time in Alaska. Alaska doesn't have lighthouses or live broadcasts. They are all computerized.

In Canada, we still have lighthouses with real people in them. They can see a black line thundering across the water and call it in. I love those people.

Sécurité translated by me means pay attention, Sécurité twice is smarten up and three times is get off the big water and head for cover, NOW!

Lorna confirms this. Pay special attention when you get up at 6 a.m. and they are already calling sécurité, sécurité, sécurité. The wind hasn't even gotten out of bed yet, just wait. You are experiencing the remnants of last night's "blow" and the best is yet to come. On this trip, EVERY morning we woke up to S.S.S. Lorna said she'd never seen a winter like it. I feel less like a wimp.

This strong woman is one of the many independent people that we have met on our travels. She talks of selling off sections of her homestead. Her daughter has left to get married in Powell River. I can tell that she misses her daughter terribly, I can relate to her. It was a feeling that I knew well, my son and daughter were miles away and there had been times that I was sure I would never see them again. It would be a lonely existence; loneliness being the worm in this breathtaking Garden of Eden. This winter of storms is taking its toll on all of us.

The next day, we opt to take a detour. Why would we want to simply take on Seymour Narrows when we can manoeuvre through four rapids instead? I am starting to figure out my Captain...when he says that "God hates a coward thing", it really means sécurité, sécurité, sécurité.

P.S. I would like to dedicate this story to my friend Donna Dorian. Like Lorna, she is a tough, independent and feisty woman. She has fought many battles and won. You will win this fight as well, girl. I think of you often.

Cries of the Furies

STONE WOMAN I

Dent, Yuculta, Green; names of rapids that you need to pay attention to. This is where you need to know about current tables as well as tide tables. The whirlpools, the sinkers in two of these rapids can get up to thirty feet across and the rapids can run 8 knots. We run at 8 knots, so you know that if we get swept up the rapids, we are NOT in control and we are NOT getting out. We have managed to navigate four rapids in a single day, which is incredible as these are best run at close to high or low slacks in the tide. This area is a little wonky, as this is where the tides meet on the backside of Vancouver Island. They are extremely confused seas and tides, leading to an even more confused navigator, me.

A monument in time, Theresa "Stone Woman" creates a masterpiece in dry masonry on a small, secluded B.C. island.

It is late in the day as we motor into the open waters of Calm Channel. We are looking for moorage. The guidebooks for boating are out-dated and the moorage that we had anticipated is no longer accepting transient boats. What to do?

Whiterock Passage catches our eye. It advises against usage without local knowledge, but the shadows are creeping down the mountains and we are getting anxious to get settled.

Whiterock Passage opens up into Surge

Narrows, beside Read Island, next door to Quadra Island. A person needs to listen to names like Surge Narrows, Blind Bay, and Mosquito Creek. Have you ever camped beside Mosquito Creek? I bet you know better now.

Range markers are navigation aids that are usually located on land. You visually line up markers that have been set up to follow the safest passage, mostly through a narrows. There may be two in front of you and two behind. You set them up as sights and have to keep them in line. Going through Whiterock Passage, there are four markers. The Captain is navigating from the saloon so as to keep an eye on the depth sounder; this area is shallow and rock-strewn.

 Problem is, he can see the markers in front of him, but he can't see the ones behind and therefore the system doesn't work. I am the range marker needle on the bow of the Audrey Eleanor. I stand with my arms horizontal and straight out from my sides, acting as a "compass". The Captain keeps me lined up and we work our way through the boulders and hidden rocks.

We pop out just before the government docks and general store on Read Island. Now, do we drop anchor in Surge Narrows, or see if we can wrangle a night at the dock? The problem at the dock is that the only space that is big enough to accommodate us is designated for airplanes. God hates a coward.

We pull in, tie up and are greeted by a smiling, diminutive lady who says the store will only be open for a short time. Her name is Theresa. They run the fridges and coolers with a generator and lights take the last bit of draw, so they shut down by dark.

The store appears to be falling into the ocean; in the dim light we notice that Theresa has DVDs for rent or trade and that a quart of milk is price-prohibitive. We swap movies, buy the milk anyway and invite Theresa down for coffee in the morning. She assures us that it's OK to stay at the dock, as the plane won't be back for a week.

The water here has an unusual quality. It is so clear that it doesn't appear to actually be there until you disturb it. It magnifies the ocean floor, which helped us to navigate the Whiterock Passage. It was time to do a little housekeeping,

Garbage disposal anywhere on the planet is an issue. Onboard and on islands, it is an ordeal. I have never believed in buying products that are processed, packaged and double packaged. This keeps waste and chemicals to a minimum. However, there is garbage, regardless. Finding areas that will even accept garbage becomes difficult, especially on the little islands. Why would you want someone else's garbage to begin with, and then you have to figure how to get it off of your island?

Small white garbage bags have cost us as much as $5.00 per bag. You get responsible quickly and start to pay attention to exactly what you are buying.

Travelling with stinky garbage attracts sea birds like crazy. They dive-bomb the boat and you get to scrub off the big white globs of recycled fish parts that they leave behind. They like to target the areas that you need to see out of or put your hands on. Our policy on what goes overboard is that, if we can eat it, the fish can eat it.

It is black, black on the back deck as I creep out to throw some soggy cucumbers overboard. I have to feel my way along the gunnels to make sure that these chunks don't end up somewhere else on the boat. The beauty of being in these areas is that there is no light pollution. I can see a very distant glow to the southwest, which I am sure is Campbell River.

The cucumber hits the water and explodes into light!! I yelp and take a few steps back…my deck swabbing brush is in its place on the back deck. I grab it and make a sweep through the ocean with it. Every bristle creates a backwash of millions of light particles UNDER THE WATER!

It's aquatic fireworks. I have never seen anything like this before, it is the most beautiful thing that I have ever seen. I yell for the Captain. My voice echoes through the darkness and I am sure everyone on the island has heard me. A grey heron squawks like what I think a dinosaur might sound like. I've disturbed him.

The Captain thinks that maybe the heron has attacked me, I am extremely excited. I truly can't get the words out, so I swish the brush through the water again. I can hear his quiet laugh; he's seen this before. After thirty-five years of diving, I expect that he has, but not me! I insist that we get into the zodiac and go for a roar (we don't row, we roar).

The Captain roars us around and around the narrows. With every oar stroke, millions of tiny florescent lights trail behind us in the sea; every water particle that drops from the oars explodes into light when it hits the ocean. The sub-surface lights are the only disturbance in the velvet black night. This is my first experience with a phosphorous bloom in the ocean, and it is amazing. The outlines of fish are becoming visible and jellyfish look better than Disney's version. What a thing!

The lady from the falling down general store, Theresa, comes for coffee and warm chocolate cookies in the morning (my daughter Kaitlin's famous recipe). There is not a lot of activity on this island. We wonder why the store is ocean bound, surely a person with lots of time on their hands would want to keep their livelihood from disappearing into the sea.

She is a very small lady, I am five feet tall and she makes me feel tall. The seclusion of the island is wearing on her. She shyly asks us if we would like to come and see her home. She takes us past the store and we walk down a narrow winding path that leads up and over huge cedar roots and stumps, we have to crawl over some especially large roots. Not sure where we are going or how extreme this is going to get, we are surprised when the dense brush suddenly opens up onto a beautiful bay.

A wide stone walkway offers easy access across the bay to the sandy beach on the other side. Curiouser and curiouser, we follow her across the eight foot-wide, dry stone-constructed walkway. When we reach the end of the walkway, she turns and smiles and points toward the hillside. As if reading our minds, she says, "This is what I do in my spare time."

The quarry-shaped hillside has been transformed into something that is reminiscent of Mayan construction. Stone staircases lead upward… (To be continued.)

P. S. Part two of this story is called Stone Woman II.

Cries of the Furies

STONE WOMAN II

In the previous Adventure, the Audrey Eleanor managed to navigate Whiterock Passage and find moorage at the government dock on Read Island. The owner of the little country store has invited the crew to come ashore and visit her island home...

Stone staircases lead upward from the rock walkway we are standing on. This is a natural basin in the rainforest that has been logged and left; now it looks like the ancient Mayans have been at work here. The basin stretches a hundred feet across and rises thirty feet upwards. The walls of the basin have rock retaining walls that layer the southeast side of it and resemble an amphitheatre from ancient times.

The walls range from a foot in height to three feet and are roughly two feet wide. These walls are all dry rock constructed; the rocks have all been set and balanced according to shape and size with no mortar. Some of the rocks weigh eighty pounds or more and have been wrenched from the earth by a leprechaun-sized lady and wrestled into place.

We stare in absolute amazement as Theresa, the tiny stonemason, repeats. "This is what I do in my spare time."

A hand-built stone staircase leads to the construction site of Theresa's new home.

In the previous adventure, I mention that her little store looks ready to slide into the ocean and that I can't understand why this should happen. There don't seem to be a lot of outside distractions to keep a person from possibly losing their livelihood due to lack of available time. It's the old partnership story. Three partners in the store with no clear definition of who's responsible for what, and so resentment creates neglect and in the end lack of communication causes destruction.

"I am Irish," Theresa declares, "and menopausal. There are no pubs close by, so to keep my sanity, I build with rock."

In over ten years of rock hauling, she has created one of the wonders of the islands. She has planted flowers and rock crawling greenery on her walls. She has a few kayak tours stop in for lunch, but nothing serious. She is ready to leave her island and make changes in her life.

Theresa's husband is milling fresh lumber to build a house. The building site sits high on a cliff that overlooks the ocean. One of Theresa's main sets of steps leads to this site, with a lookout positioned to view the dock. Her next project is to build a round rock enclosure below the lookout, close to the beach. It will create a natural pool when the tide fills it and the sun will warm the water to create a natural bath.

The house is being constructed of straight-grained fir. The wood is beautiful and of a quality that we seldom see in the Yukon. The fact that he is using this for studs and support walls that will never be seen is beyond our reckoning. We are curious as to how this will work, building using all green wood. His theory is that it is all green wood and therefore, it will all shrink accordingly. Another new concept. You learn so much when you travel.

Still in awe, we head back to Audrey. We are planning to head for Quadra Island and dock at Heriot Bay for the night. Remember the reference that I made to paying attention to the meaning of names? Well we are at "Surge Narrows", and the narrows, they are a-surging! We had dropped the prawn traps beside the local traps in the narrows the night before when we were roaring around checking out the phosphorescence.

The floats on the traps are mostly submerged and the water rushing over them is causing rooster tails that spray three feet into the air. Time to relax, we cannot control this, the sea is the master. We will wait for the tide to turn to ride it south to Quadra Island.

It isn't very far to Rebecca Spit and Heriot Bay, on Quadra Island, possibly 20 kilometres, probably less. Theresa talked about rowing her kids back to Read Island from Quadra one dark clear night. They were almost at Read Island when one of her daughters let a shriek out of her. Theresa stopped rowing and looked over the gunnels. She said that it was one of the most blood-chilling sights that she has ever seen.

A school of dogfish was following the shallow skiff that they were in. Dogfish are baby sharks in appearance and personality in my opinion. The phosphorous that seems to be prevalent in this area outlined the bodies of the fish and distinguished their features as well.

A school of hundreds of mini sharks, all glowing green in the ocean, has to give new meaning to eerie. Theresa said that they simply sat in the boat. She sat, trying to compose herself and stay calm so that she didn't transfer her terror to her children. The kids were too afraid to even talk and it felt that if they remained quiet the glowing sharks might lose interest and leave. They did not.

Finally, the cold drove her to put her oars back in the water, look Straight ahead and row like hell. They reached Read Island in record time.

This is a leisurely cruise for us. The tide has turned and we let it carry us south to Rebecca Spit. I am watching for navigational aids that will lead us safely into harbour. There is a strange line in the water leading from the spit point and going directly across the mouth of the harbour.

As we get closer, I can distinguish large logs that appear to be tied together end to end with no break in sight. The Captain slows our ship down and we approach what looks like an escaped log boom. The tide creates all sorts of "tide lines" and this is one of the most impressive ones. Huge cedar logs are lined up end to end. There is flotsam, small trees and an interesting assortment of collectibles, all hugging the big cedars that from a distance look like an impregnable barrier.

Once we get Audrey's bow up to the line, it is still formidable. We are an antique inland cruiser, not an icebreaker. Slowly we pole our way through the rubble, creeping along with out displacement hull helping us to manoeuvre through the mass/mess. A little bit of wave action helps to push rubble to the side. We break through and are on course for the private dock at Heriot Bay.

The Cortes Island ferry that travels to Whaletown is just leaving the docks; we wait for her wake to slack before we to tie up. The Canadian Coast Guard (these are great people, we appreciate them very much) are casting off and again we wait, with obstructed view. Finally, we get dockside, only to discover that the docks are on a strange angle to the boat. The docks are falling into the ocean, what's with this part of the world? Maybe Mother Earth and Poseidon are winning after all.

I have to jump five feet from Audrey's bow onto a dock that is sitting at a 30-degree angle, slanting into the ocean. Now we know why the Coast Guard left. God hates a coward. We tie up anyway.

We crosstie to the dock to try to insure that we don't leave with the evening tide. After weeks of solitude, this small harbour is very busy; there are even streetlights! Night is gently falling, the sounds of music and laughter are being carried across the sea to our boat. Lights are coming on and candles are being lit in the old inn. People are walking up to the restaurant and pub. We go ashore to see what other adventure we can find.

P.S. Mike House, my friend, I thank you for your research.

Cries of the Furies

WINTER IN DEEP BAY

Audrey is moored in Deep Bay, B.C. in the midsection of Vancouver Island. We had crossed the sandbar in front of Comox early the following day. This is a notoriously rough area, because it is shallow and the waves stack. The range markers lead you directly from Georgia Straight towards Vancouver Island. What this translates into is you taking it on the "beam". Audrey doesn't like taking it on the beam. She rocks and rolls and wants to fall on her side into the sea, known with dread as "broaching".

Winter on the water. Heavy, wet snow sinks smaller vessels.

We don't have a choice as to our approach to land. The waves are pushing 15 feet, and even higher further out. We are tired of being beat up. Our assumption was that once we were in the Vancouver Island area, the seas would be a little gentler; this would make life a little easier. Not so.

You have more protection from the open seas in Johnstone Straight. The swells don't get as big, but the winds howl down the Straights and whip the water into a frenzy of waves. BIG waves.

There is a 35 foot fishing boat trying to make it into harbour in front of us. He disappears from sight as he drops into the trough, before climbing the small mountain of water in front of him only to disappear over the top again. Oh God, oh God!

The sea is breaking over the bow, making us semi-submersible. Our bowline breaks free and slams into the fragile, almost sixty year-old front window. This isn't a good thing; the line is long enough that if it drops over the side it could end up in the propellers. The rope chooses to stay coiled on the front window, which is wonderful; I know who would have to climb up on that bucking bow to secure it. Let's get to shore already, I don't want to do this any more. Finally, the Captain is able to position Audrey so that we have following seas, much nicer. I like following seas.

Comox Harbour is considered a very desirable moorage. It is a beautiful spot. There are parks, restaurants and pubs at the water's edge; it's a story book kind of town. My son, Bob, was born here in St. Joseph's General Hospital. The town centre is very close by, so stocking up with groceries is easy. Some marinas are literally miles from supplies.

Lots of people; lots of rules. The yacht clubs are heavily regulated, we are happy to get moorage at the fisherman's wharf. (We don't own a pair of white duck pants, what are they?)

We spend a wonderful night in Comox, celebrating the Captain's birthday; dinner and dancing are the priorities. Whoever the band was, you were great! This morning's destination is Nanaimo. One of the Captain's sons lives there. I had attended Malaspina College (now known as Vancouver Island University), and left with great memories. These are good reasons to spend the rest of the winter snuggled up to Protection Island.

No problem leaving Comox Harbour this morning, and we are cruising between Denman Island and Vancouver Island. This Inside Passage will keep the icy, mean fingers of the Furies off of us for a short time, should they show up, yet again.

Audrey is slicing through the waves and we have just reached the tip of Denman when the Coast Guard weather report begins to call, "Sécurité, sécurité, sécurité"...pay attention, pay attention...hurricane-force winds are predicted AGAIN!

I am feeling that our being out here has challenged the Gods and we will pay for our stupidity. How dare we take on the sea!

This really is unbelievable. Everywhere that we have travelled, there have been hurricane-force wind alerts, rain and snow alerts, power outages with trees falling on houses and cars...what is going on? We have come all yhis way to spend a milder winter than the Yukon and Alaska would provide for us and our favourite lady, the Audrey Eleanor. So much for that theory. I had promised the Captain that southern B.C. provides warmer temperatures. Rain, of course, but no snow and a much easier winter than Whitehorse. He has stopped listening to me.

What to do, what to do? By now, we are nearing the end of Denman. Off to our right is the harbour at Deep Bay. I had been here years earlier, but not with the intention of docking or anchoring a boat of this size. We will soon find out if there is room at the inn.

The Captain swings Audrey starboard and we slow down to see what's inside. It looks to be a well-protected anchorage with two large ships secured just outside the main dock space. They would act as great windbreakers. Our bow glides into the inner harbour. We see a government dock and private yacht club...there is no room at the inn. With no choices left, we drop anchor in the very small space in front of the government wharf.

Being at anchor in hurricane winds is no fun in a big space, but this little anchorage doesn't allow for any swing room. Plus, there are boats and small docks anchored everywhere. There is some unusual activity on the government wharf; four guys are shuffling boats around on the outside edge. Miraculously, they have opened up a 55 foot space. I yell from the bow, (that's one of the first mate's main jobs, yelling), "Who's the space for??"

The call from the Harbour Master comes back, "You!"

We cannot believe our good luck. This is absolutely amazing! In Comox, we had asked about winter moorage. They had a ten year waiting list. This is a government dock mind you, but it really is a miracle. I do believe that I set a record pulling up the anchor. The Captain cruises us on over, I throw the ropes to the dockside gentlemen and they tie us up, this is surreal.

Cliff, the Harbour Master, welcomes us to Deep Bay, shakes our hands and introduces us to his crew. I asked him how long we could stay in this spot, and he replied, "As long as you like."

Wow, this is a dream. Cliff's old dog wobbles over and slobbers all over my hand, it's real. We secure Audrey for another night of hurricane-force winds. It's an early night after a late night of celebration. If there were hurricane-force winds, we slept through them.

In the morning, it's a strange light that's coming through the windows. It's familiar, but it shouldn't be in this place. There are six inches of snow on the docks. The outside sounds are muffled by a layer of insulating snow, which completely covers the Audrey Eleanor.

The bay has become a mushy mass of snow sitting on top of the salt water. There are trumpeter swans trying to push themselves to shore for breakfast. They leave dark grey water trails behind themselves in the sea. The smaller birds are simply walking on the thick water. Everyone looks surprised. A harbour seal pokes his head up through the mush and tries to maintain his dignity with a blob of slush running down his face. I doesn't work, I believe he's laughing too.

We try to open the back door to get out. It takes a few attempts as this is a little door and the snow is that thick, packing, slushy kind. This is the heavy kind of snow that adds hundreds of pounds of weight to dock surfaces and boats. Water lines are on boats for a reason, when the water is above those lines either they are taking on water, they have too much weight onboard, or both. There are lots of boats with no visible water lines.

People try to shovel off their boats with spatulas and coffee cups, small pieces of wood…remember, it doesn't snow like this in this area. Why would you have a shovel on a boat?

Audrey is sitting a lot lower in the water than usual, but this is not a worry for us at this point; this lady can handle the extra pounds. Dark falls early, and there are still lots of boats left sitting precariously low in the ocean. They should be shovelled off. There isn't enough manpower to finish the job and, incredibly, most boat owners don't show up. We have a small shovel that we use to harvest shellfish; it is now a snow shovel, the docks need to lose some weight, or they will sink as well.

The radio blares out yet again, "Sécurité, sécurité, sécurité," another hurricane-force wind heading our way with snowfall warnings. Enough already. Boats that are covered in massive pounds of snow won't make it through another blast of Old Man Winter's bitterness.

His girlfriends, the Furies, are here. They scream down the docks. CBC Radio can't compete in volume, we receive broken messages. The hatches are battened down and anything else that could become an airbourne missile is secured. What will the morning bring? The Captain readies his dive gear, as there will be ships to re-float. The lines get checked yet again, we sit in the dark and wait…. to be continued.

Cries of the Furies

DEEP IN DEEP BAY

Too many chiefs with not enough experience.

We are docked at the government wharf in Deep Bay, on Vancouver Island. The Coast Guard weather report is calling for another night of hurricane-force winds after a night of record snowfall in an area that didn't expect it.

We sit in the dark and wait, the lights on the dock fade in and out as the winds whip the power lines, causing a break somewhere in the miles of line that keep things lit up and warm. Audrey is sitting broadside to the dock. One of her greatest features is the vast amount of windows that allow us incredible visibility and sunlight when it happens.

Tonight, we hold our breath, as in the intermittent light we can see flying debris. This is a threat to that large expanse of glass. Pieces of plywood swirl up and slam against the boats and dock. Canvas covers are ripped off of flying bridges on nearby boats. Hatches and sail covers are torn by icy fingers; pieces fly skyward and are silhouetted against the strange orange glow in the night sky.

Plastic pails and aluminium cans, along with all the collectibles left from the summer become airborne missiles. The masts and rigging on the sailboats bang and scream with the Furies. This is out of our control, again we can only sit and wait.

When we fell asleep is guesswork, but we wake up to an eerie light and an amazing sense of calm. The winds have drifted the snow in on the back deck, and we have to dig our way out. The dock area is a hurricane scene. Small boats are half submerged, the dock and harbour are littered with flotsam and the swans now plough their way through slush and have to swim around chunks of wood, life vests and survival rings. The sand-pipers totter on the life rings, chirping at each other as they struggle to maintain their balance.

The work begins; trying to match pieces of canvas by color to the boat they belong to looks to be an endless puzzle. We end up by piling the canvas covers on boats that look like they might have had canvas to begin with. Cliff, the Harbour Master, shows up. He states that some of the larger boats have sunk as well. It becomes established that Audrey's Captain is a commercial diver. Cliff goes to make contact with the owners to see if Rick needs to suit up and float their boats for them.

A twenty six foot sailboat is sitting on the bottom of the bay. The weight of the snow from the previous day, in conjunction with an open seacock in the head (toilet), allowed open access to the sea and she is now on the bottom of the bay with her bow positioned partially under the dock.

This is a well-known oyster farming area; we are minutes from Fanny Bay, B.C., on Vancouver Island in Canada. Very expensive, sorted oysters have returned to the deep, hopefully still nestled in their trays. They need to be rescued. A new twenty five foot aluminium skiff with twin 250 horse engines is still tied by the bow to the dock; it is now in a vertical stand. The engines on the transom are positioned to be driven into the muck by the weight of the skiff as the tide goes out. There are countless skiffs that are half-floating or sunk, but with no engines or technical equipment, so they can wait. The Captain needs to be ten men.

The fight is on; the sailboat owner wants immediate action on his sailboat. Tom, the oyster farmer, wants his oysters rescued first. A decision is made, the Captain sends Mike, the sailboat owner, into Courtenay to buy inner tubes and other necessities to float his boat. He suits up to go oyster diving.

The dry suit that the Captain is wearing fascinates the locals. Most of them have diving experience in some form or another, but the need for a dry suit in this area is not heard of. This suit is essential for diving under the ice in the far north and south to the Antarctic. The Captain appreciates it warmth today.

Tom is pleased when his trays of oysters are returned, mostly intact. Next...the plan is to float the sailboat. The Captain has pulled small aircraft from lakes, a car from a mostly frozen river, and impressively, a water bomber from Strategie Lake in the Northwest Territories from a depth of 100 feet. This was after another dive crew had determined that it couldn't be done. This sailboat is all in a days work...or is it?

The bow is under the dock, so it will not come Straight up. The Captain's job is to raise it and Mike and his buddies will pump it out. I am the tender and surface support crew; I am the only woman on an all-man dock.

The inner tubes are positioned and inflated inside the stern of the sunken boat, so that the stern will rise and pull the bow out from under the dock. The boat is lying on its port side with the mast jutting on an angle just above one of the dock fingers. I am intent on watching the Captain; he is inside the sunken boat and I don't want any of the lines to entangle him.

Suddenly, one of the dock guys throws a hose into the water beside the boat and turns on the pump. In seconds the visibility in the water turns to churning mud. I yell at him to get the #@*#ing hose out of the water and shut the pump down, the Captain has lost his vis (visability). I look up to find Mike tying the mast of his boat to the dock; the boat has started to rise at this point. It's a gong show!

Again, the air turns blue as I yell at him to loosen the lines. With the boat rising and the mast tied, she'll end up topside with the Captain underneath. My goodness gracious, where is the common sense? I now have ten sets of angry eyes turned my way. How dare a woman tell them what to do?! The sailboat is visible, and I can see the Captain sitting in the cockpit as she slowly rises to the surface. OK boys, NOW get ready with that damned pump!

I am glad to have the Captain back beside me on the dock. I rinse him down dockside with fresh water; we assemble all of our gear and get our first real look at the sailboat. She's a pretty little thing.

The crew assembles on board Audrey for some decompression juice (beer) and to compare stories. There are several sheepish thank yous. As usual, in the end, everyone is friends after a job well-done. Mike assures all of us, particularly his boat partner, that he will make sure to secure his seacocks in the future and shovel off the boat. It was his turn to take care of their boat, lucky guy.

The aluminium skiff stayed tied to the dock through low tide. She ended up pushing her engines into the bay and snapping off her kickers; they were brand new. No one could contact the owner, and in the south you just don't touch some else's boat without permission.

The evening continues with yarn-spinning about bigger storms and more sunken boats. We lucked out when Gail Ferguson asks permission to come aboard with her guitar. With her excellent voice and incredible style, she serenades us into the night, it is magic. I think that she should do an outdoor concert at Stone Woman's place on Read Island.

P.S. One of the members of the Harbour Board clocked the winds at the dock that night at 110 mph. The power was off for four days, and the roads were mostly impassable with fallen trees and power lines. The Island Highway was a mat of fallen cedar boughs.

An older lady at the corner store in Bowser had the fortitude to have an old kerosene lamp and hand crank till, so groceries could be bought and paid for the old fashioned way; she added up your purchases with a piece of paper and a pencil, and you paid her cash. Most of the other stores remained closed because of technical difficulties (electrical dependency).

Cries of the Furies

THE PIRATES

Stern tying allows more boats per square inch, makes marinas more money, and causes mass confusion.

I remember bits and pieces of a song that go something like, "She got the goldmine and all I got was the shaft." Don't remember who sang it, or the name of the song. I recall strains of this lament drifting on the spring air after a long hard and dark winter in the Yukon.

A similar version on the docks is, "She got the house, and all that I got is this leaky boat." The twang of this seaside version sometimes swings hard to starboard, with an "I showed her" attitude, and, "I can leave this dock and conquer the seven seas whenever I feel like it." The portside position of it is: "I am in the depths of despair; I want to eat worms and possibly feed the fishes."

There are several guys singing variations of this song, living on this dock. When you watch it from across the way, it is an interesting substitute for television and Dancing with the Stars.

Living on board your boat when moored at this government dock is not tolerated; with exceptions. It's the exceptions part that is causing grief. The board members have come to the conclusion that the pirate bachelors who lived on the dock have to leave, but no one wants to be the first to show up with the eviction notices. Some of these "pirates", as they liked to refer to themselves, are on "tilt."

Surprisingly, the mornings on the docks get off to a productive start. The sound of hammers and saws mixes in with snatches of song from different boats and partial conversations float over the water to create a vibrant morning concert. Mondays to Wednesdays, things fade early in the afternoon. Thursdays and Fridays, the morning dock song starts off with a bang, but by coffee time, one by one, the members of the seaside band began to fade away.

Even immersed in eau de turpentine, I can smell something that is the "dead skunk in the middle of the road" scent. I don't believe that it is possible to hit a skunk on the sea with a boat. We are in British Columbia, the garden province of Canada, and home to B.C. Bud. The dock gets quieter and quieter, this is the best behaved these boys have ever been. The weekends are a different story, whatever they ingest revs 'em up and they don't have enough room to turn around in, much less go anywhere. The work week for the most part is three days long.

There are productive and hard working people who live and work off the docks as well. Comparatively, we have oil and water. As the newcomers, we tried to remain on the sidelines and to stay out of the way. The pirates have managed to vote one of their members to the board of directors for the dock. This is one of the reasons for the reluctance of the board to remove the pirates that are living here, onboard. This board member lives on his sailboat as well. Grey areas cause conflict.

Articles begin to disappear from the boats and dock. We watch this procedure with great interest. During the night, the gremlins went around and reorganized people's belongings. Things aren't taken for days, they keep moving closer to the black hole that opens up in the night and swallows them whole. A dinghy that has been three fingers over is moving closer and closer to the boat that represents the black hole. After a week of subtle movement, one morning the dinghy simply disappears. The rat that lives in the black hole begins to get too bold. One of the men who did actual work on the docks calls him on the disappearances. Now we have dock wars!!

The pirate rat sneaks over at night and cuts the man's ropes to his boats. The man is more direct; he takes the water hose and inserts into a vent in the rat's stern, then leaves his calling card. The card simply says, don't fool with mine or anyone else's stuff. If you do, I will turn on the water to the hose. He then signs his name and leaves his phone number. Very direct, very concise. Every coward needs to assemble an army; the rat says that he is bringing in his buddies, "The Angels". The rat is the board member, by the way.

The docks are on overload, affordable moorage is hard to find and the government docks are usually reasonably priced. They have decided that due to the demand for space they will have to stern tie everyone. We still have to pay for 54 feet of moorage, but we are actually only using 12 feet. This means that the people on the inside cannot leave the dock without moving boats to get out. We are in the centre of the dock and by golly if the pirate rat's boat doesn't get moved right beside us. His sailboat is 45 feet in length. Being this close up and personal makes it difficult to stay out of the line of fire. I am really glad that we have a direct route to the outside and can leave just as soon as the last bit of bright work is done, or sooner, if this battle heats up.

There is an extreme amount of traffic to and from the pirate rat's boat at all hours of the night. He has been retrofitting his sailboat and all of a sudden he has acquired enough money to buy himself new sails and fittings. Because we are all stern tied, his sailboat is secured to our portside. We are holding his bow into the bay and look directly into one another's windows. One of this pirate's claims to fame is his extensive knowledge of anything that floats on the water, his fellow pirates are ardent followers. The pirate rat attaches his sails and his riggings.

There are storm warnings on the radios that echo across the docks. The pirate rat thinks this is the perfect time to try out his main sails and it probably is; out in the harbour. I am hurrying to put the finishing touches on a set of stairs that the Captain has just finished building, deep in the turpentine again and dreaming about future harbours.

The swooshing sound that is lulling me deeper into daydreams suddenly registers and jolts me into reality. I am on overload with a grand dose of incredulity. The goofy bugger is raising his sails while he is dockside and still attached to us. I take off at a run, looking for the Captain, or anyone else that can stop this fool.

The Goddess comes through again, the Captain is schmoozing nearby. He returns at a run when I explain the situation. By the time we get back to Audrey, the rat is almost at full sails. The lines securing his boat to ours are groaning with the strain of remaining stationary. Our cleats remain attached, but for how long? His lines are as taut as bowstrings and he is pulling our portside into the air with the force of the wind in his sails. We are no lightweight at 30 tonnes, but against the force of the wind in those sails, we are nothing. Mother Nature will win, as usual.

"We are friends till the end and this is the end, my friend. I am cutting your lines!"

The Captain jumps to portside with his knife. Opened-mouthed, the rat instantly drops his sails onto the deck.

"What are you doing?" demands the Captain. The red-faced rat has no explanation. Now we have challenged the coward and shamed him on the docks in front of his peers.

We spent part of the winter looking for suitable moorage and when the weather lifts, we are clearing out. The honourable board members have asked us to stay on to keep an eye on the docks; the looting has slowed somewhat because there is an outside presence. There are jobs when there is nothing that can make it worthwhile, and this is one of them. There are wonderful people on the docks and a few bullies and thieves seem to dilute the good, it's funny how that works. A little poison goes a long way, the one bad apple routine.

The "Angels" never showed up and the good guys managed to run the bad ones off. I have developed wariness when I see a pirate flag blowing in the wind. It may seem a fun thing for weekend cruisers to hoist the Jolly Roger; it now represents idiots to me.

P.S. Ms. Lorraine McInroy, we have heard that you have a birthday next week; we have also heard that it is a very special one, Happy birthday!! (You won't be able to catch me, I can still run.)

Cries of the Furies

END OF THE NORTHERN ERA

Captain Doug's work tug, the "Wee Haul". We used it as a dive platform.

This is the end my friend. After hurricane lashings, cold, wet nights (the toothpaste was frozen some mornings), and dock disputes, spring has finally beaten up old man winter.

The Furies still try to push their way around the docks and stir up shorelines, but they are losing much of their ability to huff and puff and blow the boats around. The sun is shining and the dock dudes are crawling out of their bachelor bunks earlier in the day. They look like wilted dandelions that need water and sun.

By coffee break, they are showing their faces to the sun and seem to be thinking about making a contribution to this day and the world around them. By 10:30, the smell of dead skunk in the middle of the road drifts down the docks and one by one the spaced-out dudes crawl back into their bunks, not to be seen till the morrow.

The Captain has made a new set of stairs for access to the flying bridge. I have applied four coats of a two-part epoxy to these works of wonder. There is beauty in simple things; wooden steps built by a welder are a thing of beauty. We are very close to leaving these winter moorings. The old steps were a hazard and access to the flying bridge was becoming dangerous, almost the last reason to put off crossing Johnstone Straight to our new home.

Doug of the docks has several barges and tugs in this bay. He also has two ships anchored at the mouth of the harbour to Deep Bay. They have acted as giant wind breaks through this winter of storms. The Furies have actually been able to shove these big guys around. They are 120 and 180 feet in length, their tonnage is a guess; they are huge ships.

Doug asked the Captain to dive beneath the ships and move the anchors to resecure them to the ocean floor before we leave. The paycheque will help fill the tanks; Doug has been an invaluable source of information, and the Captain is happy to help. The tugs that are sitting dockside are being refurbished and will be resold. There will be one leaving shortly for Panama. We are asked if we would like to crew one. Oh my, we would love to crew one! Reality is a soul-buster. Audrey needs to be moved from this dock, we wouldn't sleep nights if we left her here. Next time, next tug.

We head out to the ships to move anchors. They are supposed to be sitting in 80 feet of water; to Doug's surprise, the Captain locates them in 105 feet of water. The hook is dropped and attached to the first anchor. The Captain plans to attach the winch to the set anchors so they can then be lifted and repositioned. This project is running smooth from all accounts on the surface; below in the dark depths of the ocean, the Captain has run into a weight problem.

While attaching the winch to the 2,000 pound anchor, the steel cable has pushed against the release on the Captain's weight belt; the belt has dropped to the ocean floor. Quick assent can be a killer at 40 feet, at 105 feet it could cause his blood vessels to explode or at the very least give him a nasty case of the bends. Years of experience diving in the icy cold waters of the Arctic and Antarctic, along with the frozen lakes and rivers in the Yukon, have prepared him to expect the unexpected.

With the sudden loss of the weight belt, the very buoyant dry suit that the Captain is wearing wants to take him topside, immediately. As the launch begins, he quickly grabs for the steel cable. Once secured, he has to climb back down the cable to search for the weight belt. After being at this depth, he will have to break his assent to the surface into several de-compression intervals in order to prevent getting the bends. He finds his weight belt, which holds him in position.

The 35 pound belt is slung over one arm and with the other he has to pull himself up the cable. You need to have both hands free in order to put the weight belt back on. The bottom of the ocean has been stirred up by the dragging anchors and cables, plus the search for the belt. There is limited visibility. With all of this action on the ocean floor, the Captain doesn't want to lose sight of the cable and get caught up in the anchors. The surface crew, excluding Doug, has little experience working with div-ers; he needs to keep out of their way and surface as quickly as possible.

Doug, the Captain of this operation, has diving experience from being with the Marines in the U.S. military. None of us are aware of the under-water drama going on. Rick surfaces a distance away from "The Wee Haul", the tug that we are working off of. Doug's face registers amazement at the sight of Rick with the weight belt slung over his shoulder. The rest of the job finishes nicely; the huge ships are now guarding the mouth of the Deep Bay harbour once again.

After months of searching for new moorage, we are extremely lucky to find our new home at Pender Harbour. We are two and a half hours away from the departure gate for Air North to Whitehorse, if we need to get home quickly. Yet, we are far enough away from the city so as not to be overwhelmed. This travel time includes the 40-minute ferry ride from Gibsons to the Lower Mainland. In the beginning, we didn't realize how fortunate we were in securing this "Venice of The North" location.

It takes two days to travel 40 kilometres from Deep Bay to Pender Harbour. I feel that Poseidon and the Furies have joined forces to keep us at dock or anchor yet again. We drop anchor in a little bay at the top end of Lasqueti Island the first night. The next morning, we head south, down the island hoping for a break in the wind; the waves are building yet again. Salty brine is beginning to break over the bow and smash against the windshield. It is time for us to hide.

In a little byte on the west side of Lasqueti, we drop anchor and shore tie to keep our nose into the waves. Slack tide shows up and allows us to "run" for the last few kilometres around the tips of Lasqueti and Texada Islands and into the snug bay of Pender Harbour. Pender Harbour is now our homeport.

This last year has been an exciting one for the crew. The Adventures of The Audrey Eleanor have grown from a three-story insert to a full year of written adventures. I hope that you have enjoyed reading them as much as we have enjoyed sharing them with you. I have learned extensively from submitting these articles. People have asked why we still continue to love our boat and the ocean after all that we have been through.

The Adventures are all true, they just didn't happen every day. There were days that slipped by with nary a whisper of wind or threat of life, thank the Goddess. What we love about the Ssea is that she is a constant teacher. You learn something new every day. It can be a cruel master, but it is a seductive mistress as well.

I can compare nothing with sitting in the hot tub, immersed in hot sea water and watching the sun set and then feeling like I'm floating amongst the stars. My Captain and partner has kept us alive through all of the Adventures. I have a deep respect and trust for him. I would sail with him anywhere and probably will. The rush of salt water against the hull and the billow of wind in the sails have anchored themselves deep in my soul. If you can't beat the Furies, you may as well hope to harness them. We may yet become blue water sailors.

People often say that we are lucky to have the lifestyle that we do. Luck has nothing to do with it. The harder we work, the luckier we get. It is a simple case of making a decision and doing it, no magic, no luck…just doing it.

The more "stuff" you eliminate from your life, the lighter you get, change becomes easier and mobility is no longer an issue. We have had many people say to us that this series has been an inspiration for them to make the decision to follow their dreams as well. I thank them for sharing that. If we can do this, anyone can, that has been my hope for these stories, to inspire people to do what they love no matter what it is. And so begins yet another chapter in life of the *Audrey Eleanor*.

P.S. This story is for our children and grandchildren. We want you to dream and then follow through and make your dreams real. Live your life; never say "I should have". Also, please quit worrying about us. Cody Magun, we are very proud of you. Congratulations on your graduation in Watson Lake this weekend, we will be watching you as you step out and begin your life. It will be magnificent!

Sunshine Coast

FROM DEEP BAY, BC TO
SALTSPRING ISLAND, BC

Find the full map here:

http://thewhitegirl.ca/stories/audrey-eleanor-map

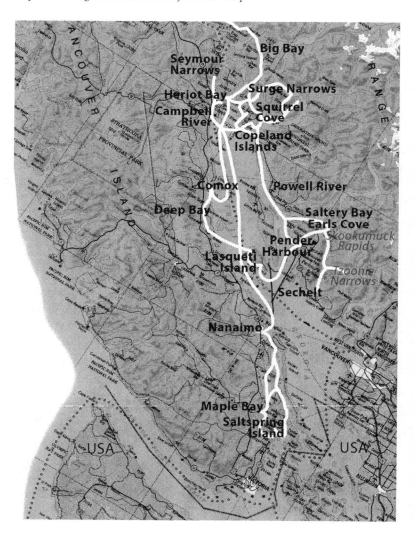

Sunshine Coast

SPRING IN THE HARBOUR

Spring is late coming to call in Pender Harbour this year. Does that make you in the north feel better? Now, you should know that by late I mean the cherry blossoms are out, but the froths of pink flowers haven't formed archways along the streets yet. This is the beginning of April. Looking up Gunboat Bay a few days ago, fresh snow was visibly clinging to the mountains as far down as I could see. The snow had almost made it to sea level, but a gentle southern breeze fluttered in and melted the "fairy dust", as I have recently heard it referred to. I am appreciating that it has left quietly and without a trace.

Spring translates into rebirth and renewal for me. The miserable snow is gone and the sun is producing life-giving heat. Maybe not enough to warm your bones, but possibly just enough to crisp your face, especially if it's reflecting back from those sheets of ice that still cling to the lake surfaces for those of you in the Yukon! Here in the Harbour, the rays are bouncing back from a sparkling ocean.

Match Cap Race (a pretend race) in Auckland, New Zealand aboard the 1995 America's Cup contender. My Captain at the helm, bringing us back into Auckland Harbour in March, 2009.

Renewal aboard Audrey means removal of old paint and varnish and strange green things that have grown up over the winter. When we first bought our boat, a fern grew in the windowsill on the dash beside the gauges at the helm. I have tried to nurture and maintain a healthy looking fern throughout a Yukon winter with difficulty and the fact that this wonderful piece of greenery simply and routinely chose our boat for its home was to me a wondrous gift.

The Captain ripped it out by its tender little roots and proudly displayed it to me, trophy-like…he could not comprehend the look of horror on my face, as my only volunteer houseplant ever lay mutilated in his hands. The fern has returned every spring since, and I now pluck the beautiful parasite from the sill. Plant growth causes wood to deteriorate.

The Captain is in the "troll hole", changing filters and maintaining his perfect Perkins engines. His engine room gleams white with cleanliness. Payback for the time he spends in the engine room is that we can turn the keys on Audrey at any time and the engines roar to life. The lines are cast off and there could be a new adventure in the making. Crossing Dixon Entrance or battling giant waves, the Perkins engines have never failed us, due to his time and care.

I am the sander/painter. One of our inside jokes is that Rick is a welder and yet he possesses a wooden boat and is allergic to sawdust. Yes, I know that an allergy specialist should certify this. I love doing the work; it is gratifying to bring back the shine on the bright work, and Audrey starts to pose in the sunshine as the grime of winter is washed away.

Lying on the teak decks with the heat of the afternoon sunshine on your shoulders is almost perfect. Having a brush full of tung oil and being able to smooth it out over the mahogany planks and expose the beautiful colour and grain of the wood…well with that and the G.U. elevens (Newfie for gull) serenading me, this is just plain heaven. I will take this over having to work inside any day.

The forecast for this Easter weekend is that temperatures should rise to 17° C with sunshine all day long. It is already 6° C at 7 a.m., so I'm thinking that we will beat that forecast today.

The hot tub is already in the water and will be floating in the sea beside the dock again today. We had a visitor the first night that we had the hot tub back in the sea. There was woofing and barking and much carrying on in the water. The sound, combined with the slapping of waves against the dock was causing us to wonder what was in the water with us.

We could not determine whether it was a curious sea lion or a sea otter, checking us out in the dark.

"Damned tourists keeping him awake at night," is what I suppose he is thinking. I just didn't want whatever was thrashing around in the ocean to join us in the much warmer hot tub. The gulls fly over the tub and seem to do a double take and come back for another look. I'm thinking we look like soup.

Spring is signalled in Pender Harbour by the white sails of the sailing clubs rounding Skardon Islands. These islands mark the inside entrance to Pender Harbour. The Islands create the perfect course for sea trials for sailboats. These boats gracefully do figure eights around each other, ocean-going ballerinas. The white sails are billowing like sheets on a line against a backdrop of a deep blue ocean and the soft green of the cedars.

This winter, we were fortunate enough to participate in a Match Cup sailboat race in Auckland, New Zealand. I had never sailed before, and wanted to experience the "other" boating style. A sailboat race was the perfect birthday gift promised for a significant birthday; although I had never expected it to happen in New Zealand. We were racing with the '95 New Zealand America's Cup contender.

The saying goes something like, "a bad boating day is a great sailing day." Well, after all of the extreme boating weather that we'd been through, I figured that if you can't beat the weather, you might as well learn how to use it. IT WAS WONDERFUL! It's like flying over the water, the 25 knot winds filling the huge sails to the limits, creaking ropes, the hiss of the water racing by. I loved it...so now what to do? So many choices. The Captain took the helm during the race and I thought he suited it very well.

I have to trek up to the Grasshopper Pub in the Pender Harbour Hotel to hit a hot spot to email this story off. Zipping over by zodiac to the Copper Sky café in Madeira Park is another great place to have a coffee and a chat with Scottie and the boys while the email heats up. But it's a tough place to get out of, and the afternoon will be biting at my heels by the time we are inspired to leave. The Grasshopper Pub wins out as the communication point of choice. The view is remarkable, and I have been watching the hillside for the resident doe and this year's fawn. The climb to the pub is extreme, but the chances of seeing the fawn are very good.

Daffodils show sunny faces on the hillside as I climb skyward to the Grasshopper. They are flashing yellow smiles throughout Madeira Park and Garden Bay. Primroses offer brilliant colours in unexpected places. The Easter Bunny will have to look for these special spots to hide her Easter eggs. The Easter Bunny hops into Pender Harbour as well as Marsh Lake, Yukon, Jianna Mia.

From my crow's nest on the deck above the marina, I can see the tide churning out of Gunboat Bay at a hard boil. When she winds up, the tide runs at about 5 knots, and with the wind whipping against her it creates a small rapid. The deceptive Woman of the Sea, at slack tide the waters are placid and create the illusion of perfect moorage. There have been a few unwary seagoers who have dropped anchor here; everyone makes an effort to warn them that they will probably be swept away at tide change. Few ever spend the night; there are nice people here. The benefits of fast water are that it flushes the bay and keeps everything sparkling clean. It also helps to prevent growth from forming on your boat's bottom and no one wants growth on his or her bottom.

Across the harbour in Garden Bay, the serious transients are already arriving. Three sailboats have dropped anchor and set up housekeeping there. By mid-summer, you could possibly walk across on the decks of boats anchored in the harbour.

A warm breeze is wafting the perfume from budding willow leaves and cedar and fir trees growing in loamy rich soil across the deck. The air is always salty; the clouds drift by in a deep blue sky. I can see the doe directly below me and what could be last year's fawn, or maybe it's a doe friend and they are out for a walk together. No new baby as of yet, it's late in arriving as well. The tinkle of ice cubes in a tall glass while sitting out on a deck overlooking the ocean is THE most definite sign of spring. Happy Easter, everyone.

P.S. Bob and Kait, I hope you have a wonderful Easter. You should be here... love from your mommy.

Sunshine Coast

MAGIC I: FLOATING UNDER THE STARS

It's time for a little magic. The end of what we thought wasn't a bad summer is drawing to a close. The locals in Pender Harbour and Madeira Park complain about climate change and in their minds, lack of a summer at all. I admit that it wasn't as hot as I would have liked it, but the days were mostly clear and sunny. Diving directly off of the dock into the ocean had happened once or twice. To the Captain's delight, some of the bar maids came down at night to skinny dip.

I finally got a chance to experiment with my new dry suit. It is a strange sight to see. Trying to keep upright and walk half-submerged around the docks causes people to do a double take when you walk/flop past their boat way out past the shoreline. We have a floating hot tub that we keep tied dockside, so if the water feels too cool for a dip we just heat her up a little. I have to say that there is nothing that compares to hot salt water for relaxing or making your skin feel like velvet. After sanding the gunnels on the boat all day, it feels wonderful.

Labour Day weekend has come and gone and so have the crowds.

The Captain and his brother, Gerry, float in the sea and sunset in Pender Harbour.

After the solitude of living and travelling in the north, the crowds are really unsettling. Desolation Sound is well-known and well-travelled by southern boaters. It's a skip and a jump for boaters travelling from Vancouver. Depending on the speed of their boats, they can get to Squirrel Cove, on Cortes Island, in a day. Pender Harbour is a natural stopover; known as the Venice of the North, it has beautiful, secure little coves, several waterfront restaurants and bars, and the "Royal" Yacht Clubs for both Vancouver and Seattle. While the club members hadn't been the most friendly of folks, over the summer they provided all of us summer locals with great entertainment.

The Royal Yacht Club ships are magnificent to watch coming into harbour, you can almost walk across this bay on anchored yachts. Dodging them with the zodiac to get to the Garden Bay Pub takes skill. We have airplane wheels on our zodiac, this makes us run a little lower in the water and we create a bigger wake then we'd like. It's slow-going, but allows for a bit of conversation with the little guys. The yacht clubs are a "members only" situation for moorage or participation. Well, when the big boys with the big flags arrive, it's like watching elephants trying to step through a field of mice and not squash them, or worse, get their feet dirty.

Consideration for fellow boaters seems to depend on size and anything below the extensive gunnels of the "Royal" yachters is almost nonexistent as they motor toward the Seattle Yacht Club. In their wake, the little sailboats truly look like pendulums in clocks as their owners attempt to maintain themselves topside with their barking miniature dogs and sloshing martinis.

Sound carries very well on water, verbal challenges charge across the harbour, flying back and forth accompanied by the scraping sound of metal on fibreglass. With the distraction by these colourful words, one skipper has forgotten that there are only two feet separating him from the boat on his portside. He now has managed to secure that neighbour's anchor line as well. The angry voices now arrive in stereo. Ah-h-h, life in the densely populated south!

The Captain is not a sport fisherman, he subsistence fishes. Isn't it amazing how really basic forms of words have changed as the lack of understanding of them grows? He fishes to feed us.

The price of a small Dungeness crab in Madeira Park is $25. The price per pound for fish of any type is out of this world; this is all incentive to go fishing. I love rockfish and have since before they became a trendy type of food. Rockfish has become trendy because of the lack of salmon, cod or halibut. I once had to process 60 lbs of hake filets that I was lucky enough to come across; it's a beautiful, delicate fish.

We spend a lovely day drifting around the small islets in the mouth of Pender Harbour, looking for rockfish. A time warp happens, six hours of floating on the ocean drifted by and we have nothing but a suntan to show for our time. It is perfect, but we really did want to catch some fish. We would obviously have to get out of town if we wanted to catch anything of a size for eating.

The timing is right. Most people should be gone, we could head for Cortes Island, circumnavigate it and do some exploring in our old haunts around Read Island…it is time to go fishing. In peak summer months, your anchorage has to be established by noon in order to find the room to set your hook. Shore tying then becomes necessary so that you do not swing into your neighbour. It is very crowded. For the free spirit, the guidebooks have listed numerous small, protected coves as anchorages. They state that these beautiful little coves will provide privacy. This is so that you need not listen to your neighbour's music or dog barking at EVERY seagull. (No, this is not so cute.)

The guide books must have been published prior to fish and shellfish farming, just about ever bay listed has now been partitioned off with nets, floats, logs and very strong. "Don't even think about getting close to us" signs…all fish farms. It's a segregated area, yachties to their space and the working fishers to theirs. Boat wakes wreak havoc on shellfish farms, where mussels and oysters dangle in the salt brine on tenuous lines.

Stories of sport fishers spending a week to get a single salmon are pretty common. They have way more patience then we do. Why oh why do we allow commercial fishing in the mouths of spawning creeks and rivers, people? If they can't go home to make babies there will be NO fish. And where is the crab? The Captain truly is the crab slayer and all summer has only produced a few small rock crabs that still needed to grow up. They were sent home to the deep to develop some bulk. We want to head into less-populated areas, where there still might be some fish and crabs left.

Audrey leaves the dock at Pender Harbour and we head up Malaspina Straight towards Powell River; Texada Island is on our port side. It's slightly breezy, but still hot enough to get sunburnt on the flying bridge. Just past Powell River and before Savary Island, I notice something strange in the water. The Captain slows us down for a better look.

Curiouser and curiouser, there is a seal in the water with a 15 lb salmon in its mouth. On each side of him are two seagulls, both determined to steal his dinner. This seal is not concerned in the least; he is more interested in watching us motor past. The gulls are playing tug of war with the salmon and he just keeps on watching us. Slowly, and seemingly without breaking the water, he sinks out of sight with his fish. It's a sign. We continue up past Lund and drop anchor in the Copeland Islands. Tomorrow, we head for Squirrel Cove on Cortes Island.

The distances here are deceptive; everything is way closer than in the north. The next morning, it only takes us an hour to arrive at Squirrel Cove. The floating bakery is closed for the season and there are two other boats already anchored here. With most anchorages in the south, you need to have holding tanks for sewage, a very good idea as I can only imagine what kind of sludge there would be in these low flushing inlets with the populations that visit here.

There is an oyster farm in here as well, regardless of the holding tank rule we decide not to buy their oysters. The two little sailboats don't look big enough to hold their crew, never mind a holding tank. Regardless, the water is crystal clear with starfish waving their arms at the oysters.

The moon is full and the stars are low enough to touch. Small lights twinkle off in the distance onboard the sailboats. We slip into our floating hot tub. The hot salt water closes over the aches of the day. A long line gets attached to the tub and we shove off into the soft darkness. Laying back, we watch the satellites and falling stars in the quiet black night drifting softly with the tide. If you reach up with your hand, I'm sure you can tip the Big Dipper and get a drink, wouldn't it be nice if it was tequila…we are afloat under the stars. (The water in the tub is really, really warm!)

P.S. This is Magic I; the next story is Magic II.

Sunshine Coast

MAGIC II: UNDER THE SEA

In the previous story, we left you while we were floating under the stars in the hot tub.

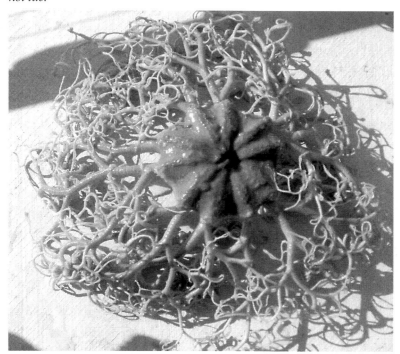

A basket starfish.

There is a small community in Squirrel Cove. The general store is well-stocked and has a decent marine hardware section. This is our introduction to "the oyster man"; he is located on Cortes Island and supplies a few of the local stores with his product, locally-grown and smoked oysters. Amazing. The cans of oysters are way too small, no matter what size they are.

We decide that we need to stretch our sea legs and walk north along the paved road that leaves the general store for other points on Cortes Island.

In the ditches, we discover the end of the summer's crop of blackberries, or brambles. I have picked these berries before. I refuse to climb down into the ditches, telling the Captain that I prefer to stay as far out the brush as I can. The things are infested with snakes...he laughs at me.

I can see this funny look come over his face as he steps further into the brambles, the thorny brush rips your skin, but that look on his face tells me that he isn't parting with his skin. I bet he has discovered the "snakes!"

Sure enough, he says, "Hmm...there are snakes aren't there." I take a stick and pull the thorny branches back; the earth is writhing with garter snakes, slithering just out of the reach of my stick.

Between us, we pick lots of berries for jam and a few extra pints get dedicated to a beautiful blackberry tincture. (Ask me about this stuff.)

There is a trail that connects Squirrel Cove to Von Donop Inlet on the opposite side of the island. We plan to anchor in Von Donop, so pass on walking the trail. We roar back to Audrey in the zodiac, pulling anchor and leaving to seek out another adventure. The water in this area has been reported to get as warm as Mexican waters; the oysters grow huge here because of it. This time of the year I prefer to laze in the hot tub.

Von Donop is a long, narrow inlet that allows you deep access into the mid section of Cortes Island. Again, we are not alone, in what is considered a late time for travel in this area. There is an eye-catching yacht, custom built in Holland, that is anchored in the centre of the bay. The lady on board this vessel is a larger-sized woman. The custom rowing skiff has obviously been built for her. She skims across the water with total ease and grace, it's wonderful to watch. She looks free and light, as she appears to escape the weight of the world.

Whaletown is our next stop. The ferry connects Cortes Island to Quadra Island at this point, and from Quadra Island the ferry connects to Vancouver Island and Campbell River.

We have difficulty setting the anchor; the bottom of this bay is all sand. The anchor sets us within talking distance of a 65 foot sailboat. Two teenage boys are swabbing the decks. They come with additional family members that total twelve. They have been living on the sailboat for two years, wintering on Vancouver Island. It is an amazing feat; they are all home-schooled by their parents. There would be no escape space anywhere onboard this sailboat with twelve people, you would be praying for good weather.

The set of the anchor concerns us, so our trip ashore is short. We are on to the next stop, Gorge Harbour. The entrance to this harbour is impressive. Narrow, natural rock face cliffs, complete with ancient rock drawings, guard the passageway. The channel opens into a large bay, the centre of which is a large shellfish farm. The sky is streaked with pinks and purples; it's time to settle in for the night.

We decide to splurge and go ashore for dinner. There is a commercial dock to portside, and with a little house beside it that has been converted into a restaurant, it looks magical. The anchor is dropped and we roar ashore for dinner. The water that drips off of the oars is glowing with phosphorous, we are leaving a trail of twinkling lights in the black water behind us. Fairy lights in the ocean are unbelievable.

Dinner is wonderful, sitting on the little deck with lights twinkling on the shore and reflecting off of the still water. The smoked black cod was the best that I've had and that means beating out the Empress Hotel in Victoria for first place. The night is so calm that the candle on our table barely flickers as it casts shadows on the wine glasses.

The next morning, we reluctantly haul anchor to cruise to Read Island. We are going fishing, after all. Evans Bay, by Read Island, is a new anchorage for us. There is a house for sale at the head of the bay; this is a sparsely-inhabited area. Once the anchor is set, however, a small boat heads our way. They are an older couple and they own the house at the head of the bay,; their house is for sale. The Captain asks about crabbing in the area, the response is that they have been here for twenty five years and there are no crabs. Damn, is there nothing left anywhere in this south country?!

The couple is heading to their winter home in Campbell River, health has dictated that they spend time closer to health facilities; this is why their island home is for sale.

The fishing gear needs to be sorted and with our heads down we don't see the tidy little Grand Banks named "HERS" approaching. There is a persistent knocking on the hull, up come our heads as the visiting Captain hands over a large slab of cod.

"Hope you like fish," he says. "Just caught it this morning."

He also is heading for Campbell River to pick up his wife, after all the boat is "HERS". They live in Los Angles, but keep their boat moored in Seattle. Business brings them to Seattle often, so they keep moorage and use HERS as their floating apartment while they are there. Holidays simply mean cruising away from the dock. I'd never thought of Audrey as waterfront property on the Sunshine Coast, it was a different perspective.

Following his directions, we set out to become the fish slayers. On the first cast, the Captain lands a two pound sea perch, good, that's supper, but not so. He says it's bait for the "big" one. Yeah right; it would have to be a giant to chase that bait. It is a giant; the cod that almost immediately swallows this perch looks too big to pull into the zodiac.

Have you seen the size of the heads on those things?! He's going to eat us. The cod is four feet long with an overgrown head; the cod head will be crab bait...what the heck, you never know till you try, right? That is, if we can fit the head into the crab trap minus his cheeks. As the giant cod is gaffed and held to the side of the boat, he lets go of the perch. The perch executes a mighty twist, wrenches the hook from his mouth and swims away. Perfect!

The sky is red this evening, and a strange light is reflecting up from the depths of the ocean. We decide that we will watch for the evening star from the front deck. The dimming switch on the stars is being turned up, brighter and brighter. Thick, billowing rain clouds are building and rolling towards us. As the evening skies darken, eerie lights start to appear in the black water. My favourite! There is phosphorous here.

Jellyfish show up first, outlined in electric blue and pulsating. Now we see tiny flickers of darting light, as tiny and usually translucent bugs begin to appear. There are outlines of fish darting after the bugs. They show up as submersed comets in the water. The ocean is pulsating with millions of flickers and streaks of light-lined creatures. The sensation that the ocean is breathing intimidates me; the whole sea is boiling with life, it is a living entity. Millions of creatures are now visible to the naked eye; the thought of swimming in this soup of life makes even the well-seasoned diving Captain think twice.

The rain hits in huge drops.

Now, we are at Disneyland. The giant raindrops hit the water and explode in a million reverberating droplets that burst into showers of light. The hills and bay are glowing in green light. Creatures below the surface appear to be swimming in thickening lime Jell-O. Torrents of rain bounce against the surface of the ocean and we are driven inside. The pounding raindrops flash back green light and illuminate the saloon… this really is magic!

P.S. We did catch three edible-sized crabs in our trap; they had a tight squeeze getting in beside that cod head. Attached to the bottom of the trap was a basket starfish; we had come across these outside of Haines. I am glad that we had seen this before. After last night, we might have thought that we'd captured a sea-going alien.

Sunshine Coast

PENDER HARBOUR WOODEN BOAT SHOW: A SPECIAL EDITION

YOU MISSED IT! Any event that is held in Pender Harbour shouldn't be missed and that is especially true of the wooden boat festival!

The **Audrey Eleanor** *is tucked in beside Don McKenzie's yellow accented tug, the Kinnard. The* **Audrey Eleanor** *won the award for best-built custom yacht at this boat show in August, 2009.*

Still intimate, but with a broad spectrum of participants that provide incredible variety, this wooden boat show allows you personal access to most boats and their owners. Translated, this means that in the park, at the marina or any of the social events surrounding the festival, you still remember whose boat belongs to who and they, in turn, are eager to discuss any aspect of the boating world and, particularly, their boat. And as age and memory dictate, they remember you as well (after the age of 40, we all need name tags).

People in brightly-coloured summer clothing line the dock beneath fluttering flags. The mood is festive as they discuss which boat is their favourite and line up to watch the ROV and hard helmet diving demonstrations. We are rafted to the "Kinnaird", a tug that is captained by Don McKenzie. The crew aboard the Kinnaird is doing the heavy hard helmet demonstration in the blistering heat of the mid-day sun.

Even with ocean breezes, the decks and docks are too hot for winter-tender bare feet. I can not imagine sitting patiently in a heavy oiled canvas suit while all of the belts and lines are connected and then… having a fifty pound brass and glass helmet literally screwed onto your shoulders while you bake in the sun.

I watch as the diver ponderously clomps in his weighted boots to the edge of the dock, and the steps that lead into the cool blue waters. The control of this man is amazing to me; at this point, I would have thrown myself overboard and drowned just to escape the heat. This may have something to do with the "power surges" I've been experiencing lately; a sudden rise in body temperature which dictate a total lack of patience and control.

Deep breathing auxiliary engines aboard the tug lulled us to sleep last night in the humid summer heat. Crew members and participants in the show sit in folding deck chairs, dockside, trying to escape into the small shadows that the house of a boat casts over the wharf. This only brings seconds of relief from the blazing sun. Below all of us is a sparkling blue ocean; the updraft of winds brings with it breaths of cool air and the scent of underwater gardens.

We drove from Whitehorse to be part of this wooden boat festival, we've never been to an actual boat show/competition before and this is the one that we feel will be the most fun. The summer has been exceptional in Whitehorse, but the scent of decaying marine life beckons to me in my sleep and our old friend Audrey sends out physic messages of invitation. We are torn continuously between the Audrey Eleanor and the Yukon.

Part of our drive takes us through Lillooet, B.C., at night. I notice lights at the peak of the mountain that poses as a backdrop to the town. My impression is that a ski lodge has been lit up for a celebration on top of the mountain. Lights are evenly-spaced and lead the way down the mountain toward the town. I have to admit that I felt envious at the thought of joining my imagined party on the mountaintop. The cool mountain breezes and the scent of spruce and tamarack would drift over us as we perused the valley below with wine glasses in hand. We have been driving for two days in 30° C heat.

As we clear the town, looking for an overnight camping site, the mountains to our right are haloed in a red glow. The scent of wood smoke grows stronger, as does the fiery glow. We round the corner to a full-on forest fire. My mountaintop party is a forest fire.

Captain Rick pulls the truck over to the side of the road and the lights are killed. Hidden in the shadows are people, silently watching as the flames spiral and explode the treetops into torches that illuminate the night. The air is heavy with uncertainty and the crackles of burnt trees are flickers of hot fingers strumming on already taut and drawn nerves. They wait to see if their town will burn. Not a word is spoken.

The Captain determines that we should head off into the very black night; this fire is burning down the mountain, which is very unusual, and not a place to be. Pemberton is not far off; we hope this will be far enough away from this terrible danger. We sleep by a roaring river instead, with stars lighting up the massive treetops instead of flames.

Pender Harbour is a most welcome sight. There is our lady, still at berth and waiting for us to board. The smell of old boat and salt water is engulfing. We feel like we are home. All hatches and portholes are opened to let any available air circulate. At three in the afternoon, the heat becomes overwhelming. Water, water everywhere! I have wanted to dive off of this boat forever, the summer heat had just never happened and I sure as hell wasn't going to do it in Haines, Alaska.

This is it, summer is here and I will dive off of our boat into the cool blue ocean. As usual, I am covered in paint and it will take too long to change into a bathing suit; I do the iced tea commercial. I am enveloped in the beautiful, cool, soul quenching water. My skin is sucking at it hungrily. Back stroke, front stroke, dog paddle, so light and free and cool, bliss. It's time to get out, I am getting tired.

Wait, there is no out. There is no ladder, and the dock is too high. The swim grid on Audrey is suddenly out of reach, it's too high. I CANNOT PULL MYSELF OUT! The zodiac, that's how I'll get out. I climb up the kicker and try to swing my leg over the side...I slide down the shaft. One time, two times, five times and with not much left to give, I manage to get astride the zodiac...we will have to get a ladder. The insides of my legs are purple and bruised for days.

At the wooden boat show, the heat is sending people for cover. I don't know about you, but I've missed summer for the last two or three years, I don't want to have to hide when it finally shows up. Let's swim! I have learned my lesson; I'm looking for ways to get out of the water before I get in.

Don McKenzie kindly offers to lower a dive ladder, so that I can get back on the dock/tug. The Captain jumps overboard, and I follow. Soon, kids jump and reappear, bobbing between the bows of the boats. Adults belly flop with a flourish; the dogs don't want to be left out either.

Kids are jumping and diving from boat bows, as their confidence grows so does the height they jump from. This friendly group of boaters is enjoying the entertainment the children are providing. Applause is heard for an especially good belly flop. There is a steady stream of young at heart people climbing up Don's ladder only to jump; just one more time.

Music is drifting over the water, people are milling and chatting. The "Gargoyle" won the people's choice award for this year, and so he should. He built his sailboat from the logs up, and she's beautiful.

Proud owners of everything from converted fish boats and plywood constructed skiffs to the magnificent "Fifer Lady" and the glorious little "Sweet Pea" all open their hatches and welcome the crowds aboard. Scents from the BBQs topside and wonderful pancakes at the pancake breakfasts all lend to the ambience of this wonderfully-relaxed and well-organized event. We will be back next year.

The Captain of the Kinnaird heard that that we planned to take on the world famous Skookumchuck Rapids the following day and volunteered to guide us through. Thanks to Kurt and Janine, we have babies on board; the infamous Jianna Mia (Made in Alaska) and her new baby sister Jessi had decided to join us. They brought their parents and

Grandma Trish along only as providers of food and a source of entertainment.

We were taking no chances on running these huge tidal rapids for the first time with this precious cargo. With Don McKenzie in the lead, we make it safely into the inside sea and the harbour at Sechelt. Thank you, Don.

P.S. We had the engines running and were dropping off our last bit of garbage at the dock when someone yelled, "Hey you guys can't leave yet, you have won an award!" Proudly we accept the honour of BEST BUILT CUSTOM YACHT at the 2009 Sunshine Coast Wooden Boat Festival.

Sunshine Coast

INVADERS

The saloon onboard the Audrey Eleanor prior to the invasion. They left nothing untouched.

Intrusion, invasion, attack, and violation. Under the cover of darkness, they creep over the gunnels and crawl into the bowels of the Audrey Eleanor. It is apparent that they have settled in and been onboard for possibly months. Access was gained on the aft deck, sneaking into holes that were gnawed through the walls. A tarp hid them from daylight and possible discovery. Once entry was gained into the hold, they proceeded to chew through the interior walls of the house and to slither into every aspect of our lives onboard our beloved boat. By the time we arrived for our summer get away, this was their home. We were the intruders, and they possessed the Audrey Eleanor.

Rats! I have never had the misfortune to set eyes on this type of vermin. We don't have the plague-ridden miscreants in the north. My knowledge of rats was of spring hunts in the Northwest Territories. The villages evacuated for weeks in early spring, as everyone headed out in search of fresh muskrat meat and hides. Rat canoes were constructed specifically for rat hunting. Sometimes built of little more than canvas over large willow ribbing, these topless kayaks were only large enough for the one person who paddled quietly through the willows looking for "rats".

The Captain had constructed ventilation covers for our portholes. Condensation in empty boats causes considerable damage. It is possible for it to "rain" in the house of the boat if there isn't enough air exchange to reduce the moisture. Heat can add to the problem. If there is minimal heat in the boat, the hot/cold exchange simply exacerbates the situation. You either have the furnace blazing or the breezes breezing. Who is foolish enough to leave a boat for the winter with a single heater going? With this new system, we were expecting to arrive and then simply head off into the sunset, no worries of condensation and mould this year.

Rats had not invaded Audrey because of our new ventilation system; they invaded just because they could. Our moorage below the hotel in Pender Harbour had gone up in price and down in service. Initially, the owner walked the docks to ensure that all lines were secured and that everyone was tucked in for the winter. We lost that lady to marriage and a new life; we wish the very best for her and I hope that she is happy. The management of the docks was passed over to a relative who refused any responsibility except for the collection of currency.

More wharfingers than not take pride in the safety of their docks. We have fond memories of Bob, the Harbour Master in Haines, declaring that no boats would ever sink on his dock. There is pride in this, a respect for themselves and the boats in their care. There is none of this on this dock at the foot of the hotel. An 85 foot ex mine-sweeper has been docked beside us for a couple of years. The Emerald Tide has no redeeming qualities as far as I can see. The sale of this tub has gone sideways, and now the courts have been left to decide her fate. In the meantime, an anonymous party is paying cash for her moorage My assumption is that the new proprietor is receiving approximately $650.00 per month for the moorage of this ...I have a difficult time even referring to her as an boat. There are 12 other motor vessels moored at this dock at any given time. There is no consideration of the other boats; we are all sold out for $650.00 per month.

Divorce causes a minimum of one year of insanity in my opinion and depending on the length of the relationship, I allow one year per five as a general rule for the insanity plea. The Emerald Tide had been purchased by an oil field worker out of Alberta to go along with the new Hummer and Harley that he purchased right after his divorce. 85 feet of party boat was his intention. I am calling him Fred. Fred determined that 85 feet of rotting planks and rusting systems were out of his league a few months into his rental purchase agreement on the Emerald Tide. (What else did he discover onboard?)

He left. I mean, he really left. He unplugged our boat initially to plug two of his cords into the station, then forgot to plug us back in. He left food on counters and in cupboards, half-spilled bottles of alcohol on the floors and both doors were wide open as an invitation to anyone and anything. A smell of decay and destruction wafted over the dock. Another smell that I now know as rat crept slowly down his gunnels and began to spread over the docks.

I wait expectantly at the saloon door for the Captain to unlock the doors to begin our summer holiday. We are looking forward to seeing how the ventilation system has worked over the winter. Spring clean up is usually two days of airing out mattresses and rugs and wiping down all systems, sometimes throwing out the odd mushroom that has sprung up in a dark corner. This new system was supposed to eliminate most of this chore.

The Captain has a strange look on his face.

"Did it work?" I ask.

His voice is unusually quiet; he says, "I think we have bigger problems."

"What do you mean?" I am trying to look over his shoulder into the dimly-lit saloon.

'Something has come aboard, it's pretty bad," he states. I can smell it, rotten and vile with a sickly sweet undertone. What on earth is it? He is scaring me; nothing scares him. He looks at me and steps to the side so that I can see inside the saloon. What could have done this?

Piles of foam chips, toilet paper, shredded rugs, black "pellets" are deep across the chart table. These are not little mouse turds and there are syrupy puddles are on the floor. The smell is nauseating; we instinctively cover our mouths…my God, is it still aboard? We don't know yet what has done this. Otters are totally destructive; mink seem to make nests on boats but leave for food and other necessities. This doesn't smell like otter. Neither one of us has ever smelled anything like this.

"Let's get out of here!" I am panicked; what ever it is might still be aboard. What is it?

The Captain says quietly again, "I think it's rats and they are still here."

I'm out of here, now! We are now both standing on the dock. What to do, what to do? At this point I truly want to burn the boat. The saloon is the only part that we have seen and the destruction and waste are overwhelming. It is the 13th of July and we have been told to be off the docks no later than the 15th of July. Expectations were to arrive with two days to tune up the engines, fill the fuel and water tanks and hit the high seas. Right now, we don't have a place to sleep.

Our relationship with the new proprietor deteriorated drastically in the early spring, when a friend called to tell us that our boat was unplugged and by all indications had been unplugged for at least three months. When we inquired about the situation, the proprietor told us this was our problem and that we would still be charged $55 per month, regardless of whether we had used power or not.

It is to Audrey's credit that she maintains a relatively dry hull. Thank the Goddess that this was not the heavy rainy season, the hull could fill up with run off from rain on the decks; she takes on virtually no seawater. This did flatten our batteries; we maintain a huge battery bank for our 32-volt system. We have two days to clean up the disaster and leave the docks. To take this plague to another dock is out of the question…hurricane winds and 18 foot waves have not taken this kind of toll on us, this is our darkest hour onboard the Audrey Eleanor…talk to you next week, this still upsets me. Part two of this story is called RECLAMATION.

P.S. This makes me smile. You were introduced to Paly Rainbow Song in the story RAINBOW SONG ON SALTSPRING. My apologies, he is Palu Rainbow Song. You can find more of him on YouTube under Days of our Lives and his name…he sings songs about this soap and is supposed to be the third most popular site in Canada…only in Canada, eh! (We are so cool)

Sunshine Coast

RECLAMATION AFTER RATS

The Captain, Rick Cousins, lies on the floor, exhausted. What do we do?

Where to start? The rats have run rampant onboard the Audrey Elea-nor for two months, we estimate. We call our neighbours who own the Knotty Gal; we want them to be aware that there are rats on the docks. As we walk, the dock rat signs are everywhere. Hopefully, few have managed to gain access to the interiors of anyone else's boat.

Holly, who owns the Knotty Gal, knows about the rats; they saw signs of them in late May. They had notified the manager of the marina and they had expected him to let everyone else know about the infestation. He was already aware of the situation at that time and claimed that a fish boat had shown up and infected the docks in May.

It is JULY 13th, we had talked to the manager several times between then and now, and he said nothing about rats! I believe that they came off of the Emerald Tide, the old mine sweep that sags at the dock beside us.

When the previous owner ran away in a hurry, he left a month's worth of food on countertops, in cupboards and on the floors. In his haste, he left both doors wide open...he was involved in a rental purchase agreement for this tub and I think he smelled a rat. Possibly several dozen rats!

Moorage on the Emerald Tide was being paid in cash until the courts could settle the rental purchase dispute. For an estimated $650 a month, the whole dock was compromised. The bilges on this boat run at an alarming rate, the weight of this 85 foot tub, in combination with the tidal current, could sink the whole dock if it went down.

Both doors left open to this vessel are an invitation for habitation by otters or mink. It had been left fully-furnished with all electrical systems still onboard, a thief's delight. Prevention is something that we strongly believe in; the Captain goes aboard the Emerald Tide to secure the doors as best he can. The aft door remains closed, the starboard side door refuses to stay shut and blows open every chance it gets...this is a welcoming invitation to any thief. This door parallels our saloon door. There has been no thievery in this area as far as we know, and we would like it to stay that way.

Come to think of it, the doors have been left open for months on the Emerald Tide and even the otters have not moved in. Why? We need a place to sleep for the night; it definitely can't be inside our beloved ship. There are two foam mattresses in the truck that will work, and we sleep under the stars on the flying bridge. In the morning, we will take back our ship.

We roar over to LaVerne's in Garden Bay for breakfast, she makes wicked good bacon and eggs. The list of necessities starts with rubber gloves and face masks. Filling up the back of our truck begins, mattresses, rugs, clothing, crab traps, fish net, life jackets, and rain gear. Rubber boots have holes chewed in them, along with a chunk gnawed out of my brand new dry suit for diving. I can't believe that they chewed up all of the Canadian Tire folding chairs, that's just mean. Kurtis bought us those last year.

All cans of food have been peed on and are rusted from urine, I had flour in a recycled drywall bucket, the thick heavy plastic containers that you can't open. Rats chewed the rim right off of it. What freaked me out was my linen closet. They had chewed through the walls of the back deck to gain access. Then, while trapped in the hold, they chewed through the house walls to get into the main living area. When I open the linen closet, I can see six large, round areas where they tried to chew through the solid plywood to get inside. My skin crawls as I think of it, their aggression is unbelievable

Buckets of bleach, buckets and buckets of bleach! Bleach now smells like rat to me. When I was a young girl on the shores of the Arctic Ocean, we had honey buckets. Pails with a heavy-duty garbage bag lining them; this was our toilet. The more you used them, the worse they smelled. Pine Sol was used to try to keep the odour under control, but it doesn't work. Now, I am reminded of honey buckets whenever I enter someone's house that has cleaned with Pine Sol. Every time I bleach my whites, I will now be reminded of rat.

The Captain sets traps. The main nest is under the wall by the chart table, I refuse to go into the foc'sle. They have freeways between the walls, I can hear them. They are so aggressive that when I walk from the saloon into the galley they slither behind me under the chart table. When I turn on them they run back into the wall. I never get a clear look at them.

After another night of semi-sleep on the flying bridge, the Captain heads below to check his traps. He has one. In disgust, he opens the saloon door and throws the rodent, still in the trap, on the dock .The question of course is, how many are there?

Sunshine is streaming in through the saloon door. I decide to be brave and walk past the chart table on my way dockside. I am in such a hurry to get past the chart table that I don't look outside, they will not control me. I jump for the dock.

Lying right between my feet on the dock, still attached to the trap, is the biggest rat that I never want to see. Yes, I screamed and then…I screamed again.

I've had enough. The Captain refuses to burn the boat; I am deadly serious about cremating the little bastards. I am out of here, enough is enough! My love affair with the Audrey Eleanor has come to a fierce and sudden halt. OK, OK, we won't burn her, but we will sell. It's agreed, but we still have to go back inside and deal with the rats…I say that we could just give her away, as-is, where-is. No more rats, I can't deal with them anymore. I mean this, this day I would give the Audrey Eleanor away. You should have been there.

Captain Rick is a sweet-talking man, God, he's good at it. I am ashamed to say, I get back on the boat. I fill up another bucket with bleach, I wash away more rat pee. This is our last day at the dock, it is beginning to rain. Tonight, we will have to sleep inside. I am physically sick at the thought of sleeping inside with the rats all night, in the dark.

Beside my face in our bunk is a fancy little vent cover with ornate metalwork. There had been a heating system in the walls at one time. I am trying to imagine myself anywhere but where I am right now. I am chanting in my head. I can still hear them; they seem to pause to look through the vent cover as they scuttle by my face.... SNAP, another one bites the dust and another one's gone. Hey I'm gonna get you too! A little Queen to break the tension.

This one isn't going down without a fight. The trap is smashed against the floor and we can hear him hurling himself around the floor in the saloon. Die already, you varmint, please. It sounds like the death throes of an alligator in the still black night. How big is this vile vermin? The one on the dock was huge, at least by mouse standards, which are all that I have to go on. I am sure they would kill a cat; they are almost the same size. Yes, they do so have that naked skin tail, very gross. It gets quiet, thank God, thank God, I mutter.

The Captain heads out to dispose of his prey. He is taking longer than I think he should. What now? He is slow to return to our stateroom and when he enters, his head is hanging a little low. I wait for the bomb to drop.

"It got away", he says quietly. I don't like it when he gets quiet. "It must be mortally wounded...it left a puddle of blood on the saloon floor."

Tomorrow, we leave the dock for somewhere, where do you go with rats? We will not share this pestilence with another dock...we drop our anchor in Garden Bay and try to resolve this terror. Us versus the rats, one is wounded, do they get mean like a wolverine when they are wounded? We will float on the seas until the rats are all dead or I am checked into the psychiatric ward... there is a "For Sale" sign on the Audrey Eleanor this day.

P.S. I know we could have checked into the Sunshine Coast Resort. Ralph would have found us a comfy room, but then I would have not had this story to tell you. Like the Captain says, if you don't do anything, then nothing happens. In hindsight, I would have gone to see Ralph.

Sunshine Coast

RAT RELIEF

ANOTHER ONE BITES THE DUST! ANOTHER ONE'S GONE AND ANOTHER ONE BITES THE DUST!

The Audrey Eleanor leaves Pender Harbour in search of a new home.

The Captain has trapped one more of the plague-carrying varmints that we picked up while being on a dock below a hotel in Pender Harbour. Rats! This word alone conjures up images of black, menacing figures that slither around corners and climb onto perches above your head so they can jump on your shoulders and bite your ears.

Rat smell is exclusive to these animals and, once known, you will never forget it or fail to recognize it if you have the misfortune to encounter it again. I was amazed where I got whiffs of eau de rat over the rest of the summer. I sniffed rat in places you don't want to hear about.

Audrey Eleanor and the remnants of her crew are at anchor in Garden Bay, in Pender Harbour. Remnants, because I am not sure that I am intact at this point. This is the second rat that the Captain has captured. How many are left? There is concern that a mortally-wounded rodent is withering in the hold, biding his time until he can attack us in the black of night. He received a serious blood-drawing bite from the trap, but escaped. The second catch shows no signs of being previously wounded. We have no idea how many we have yet to kill.

Queen's song *Another One Bites the Dust* becomes my mantra. There has been a shift in control since my wonderful man killed the second beast, I can feel it. While I still hear a rattle here and a scuttle there, they (or it) are now afraid. We are the hunters now, not the hunted. As I stomp the decks reclaiming my home, "Another One Bites the Dust" is my war cry.

A decision is made to leave Pender Harbour for Brown's Bay Marina. Brown's Bay is located JUST at the north end of the famous Seymour Narrows. Captain George Vancouver in 1700 described Seymour Narrows as one of the vilest stretches of water in the world. On April 5, 1958, the largest non-nuclear explosion to date blasted Ripple Rock into fragments. This rock was a deadly obstacle in Seymour Narrows. The explosion pulverized 370,000 tonnes of rock and displaced 320,000 tonnes of water. This was one of the first pieces of CBC coast-to-coast live coverage ever done in Canada. Ripple Rock is gone; Seymour Narrows still commands respect, Ripple Rock collected an estimated 110 lives during its reign of sea-commanding terror.

Audrey has no home. We need to find moorage that will ensure her safety and not break us financially. She truly is amazing, asking very little in return for what she has given us. Mike, at Brown's Bay, is an ex-bush pilot from the north. He invites us to come and give Brown's Bay a look-over. If it works for all of us, this could be Audrey's new home.

Cortes Island is en route to Brown's Bay, sort of. We decide to spend the night in Gorge Harbour and relax. It is quiet onboard.

Gorge Harbour is home to the Floathouse Restaurant. They have the best smoked black cod in the world, according to me. We anchor out and take note of our surroundings. This is the only bay that we have ever drug anchor in during the night. The third week of July means crowded harbours; we finally drop the hook between two southern big boys with even BIGGER flags. My goodness, we know where they are from; they must have to continually remind themselves.

Dinner is wonderful; we sit out on the deck and watch the golden globe drop below the deep green of giant cedars. Our waitress regales us with stories of living with her son on a derelict sailboat in Belize. I could listen to her all night long, people have the audacity to demand their dinners, she has to leave. It takes courage to live her life and she has our admiration. This conversation validates our lifestyle, and instead of being consumed by rats I start to remember all of the wonders that we have seen while onboard Audrey. From Alaska to Vancouver Island to the Sunshine Coast and many, many islands in between…we have been fortunate!

Winds begin to build in this harbour. Nor'westers have restricted boating this summer. We are sheltered in this harbour, and while the Furies start to misbehave, we feel relatively secure. Shrieking and howling with no manners at all, these ladies of windy misfortune cry us to sleep. But, of course, something is wrong. I wake to the sound of water rushing down the sides of the boat. I look out into the moonlight. We are now up close and personal to one of the big U.S. ships, they come from the land of lawsuits, you know.

Anchor dragging is the dread of any boater. Not again, why, in this harbour?? Clouds have suddenly covered the moon and visibility is non-existent. The Captain starts the engines. We don't want a collision with the plastic yacht. Boats are sailing past us in the dark; the other big-mouthed ship from the south is hammering on its horn, of course this helps. Shattered skippers with shattered nerves are already doing their best. A tiny sailboat just misses colliding with the big mouth; I wonder if the crew are awake or even aware of dragging, this is danger.

The Captain is trying to reposition us in the screaming black; sheets of rain are stopping lights from penetrating the dark. We have edged forward and are trying to drop the hook between two sailboats. They are secured to mooring buoys, we should try these sometime. I sweep our spotlight between the two boats forward, trying to give the Captain some bearing. The Furies threaten to rip me off of the bow. The Captain secures us. At one point, we are within boarding distance of a large sailboat. Too close, too close!

SNAP…as I fall into the saloon, the rat trap is sprung. Another rat bites the dust. I am sure it decided to become a kamikaze rat; you need to have real stuff for this kind of life. Falling into our bunk, we don't care. The morning will come way too soon.

Sunrise is spectacular. It often is after a storm, the promise of a beautiful day wipes out the terror of the night before, reminds me of childbirth. Another rat is thrown overboard; we are hoping this is the last. The holding ground in Gorge Harbour is sand, there is nothing to secure the anchors. This is the reason why our 30 tonnes drag here.

Onward to Brown's Bay. Rounding Cape Mudge, with Campbell River resting above the beach, the ocean is flat calm. We have to wait for a flood tide to carry us through Seymour Narrows and into Brown's Bay. It is early in the day, so we decide to explore the west side of Quadra Island.

Famous April Point is to our starboard side. We nose into the ferry wake as tourists wave to us while they cross between Campbell River and Quathiaski Cove on, Quadra Island. What is Gowlland Bay like? The chart shows a large harbour and the boating guide states that it has a good holding bottom, mud with sand closer to shore. This is noted as a good holding position for ships waiting to traverse Seymour Narrows at the right tide and current.

Oh my, Gowlland Bay reminds us of tropical paradises that we have visited and wished we could move to. This one's in Canada, eh! Sandy beaches and turquoise waters. Seals with big, limpid eyes break the still surface of the water, and if you blink, they disappear. Temperatures are reaching into the early 30's; there are only two other boats in this bay. Children from one ship have gone ashore and are splashing in the shallows. We have three hours to wait for the tide change and the charge into Brown's Bay.

What do you think? Mañana, today we will splash in the ocean, drink beer and lay naked in the sun. We believe that we have now killed all of the rats; we have finally secured our ship. The Adventures of the Audrey Eleanor continue.

P.S. As I gracefully grow older, I no longer believe that time heals all. I do believe that time rubs down the sharp edges of recollection, which enables us to continue on with our lives. No, I am not over rats yet, but I am accepting the rays of light that glimmer through the cracks in my rat armour, remembering why I loved our lives aboard this beautiful ship. (It could just be the beer talking.)

Sunshine Coast

ENCOUNTERING THE ROBERT S

1942 Ex-gunboat, the Robert S.

Well, hello there, how are you doing, my it's been a long, long time…how are we doing? Well, I guess we're doing fine. Our adventures are sounding like an old country western song. Do you remember my mentioning that a person should pay attention to signs, gut feelings, or places with names like Mosquito Creek and why would you camp in such a place? In this series of adventures we will come back to that…in the meanwhile, it has been a long time since we've chatted. I hope that all of you are healthy and happy.

We are sitting dockside at Cameron Island in Nanaimo, B.C., Canada. It's a blustery Saturday afternoon. We are sipping cold beer and visiting with one of the Captain's sons and his almost daughter-in-law. The Captain's youngest grandson, Chayce, is playing in the sunshine on the floor of the saloon.

Over the adults' conversation, a two year old's version of motorcycle engine noises rises and fades as he climbs huge mountains with his "Harley". It is a peaceful scene.

The wind has blown us sideways all summer. This afternoon, the dock is filling up as the "G" forces of Mother Nature are being felt on the ocean. Boats are returning to the safety of the harbour in the face of yet another "blow".

There are a hundred feet of empty dock in front of us. We have come in to tie up, safe and secure. Anchorage by Newcastle Island, in front of Nanaimo, is mostly filled with boats, all the way to the rim of rock that surrounds the harbour.

Audrey had initially deked through the smaller boats and managed to set anchor in amongst the bobbing colours of boats as they pranced on the seas in front of Protection Island. I watch the rode (rope that holds the anchor) to see if it tightens up as the Captain slides the engines into reverse to try and set the hook. It doesn't seem to catch, the line tightens and then slackens off and tightens again…we are bouncing off of the bottom. We begin to drift.

We are becoming too familiar with the shiny white Nike (some of these white plastic contraptions resemble the newer design of running shoe in my wondering mind) to our starboard side. This particular boat is sporting a flag with stars and stripes on it that I swear is longer than the boat. They are trying to appear nonchalant, as Audrey's 30 tonnes closes in on them.

Their little dog is barking nervously. I think that I should begin barking myself. Our windlass is stripping out every time that I try to crank the chain up from the bottom of the sea.

The Captain leaves the helm to see what's up. The gear has stripped out in the windlass, and it will now take the two of us to pull up the anchor. With both of us on the bow, there is no one to take the helm. Staccato barking from this rodent-like mutt is now ricocheting off of my forehead.

My last, last nerve is hanging there like a thin icicle, someone is sure to get too close and it will snap. This shiny boat could be the snap; they have begun to lower their dinghy in anticipation of a collision. What they don't realize is that the Captain works best under pressure. He now becomes two people; helmsman and windlass stabilizer in the same instant. I am just trying to inch the damned chain in and not pay attention to the rest of the catastrophe. My heart can't take it. Breathe, just breathe.

I can see the anchor. The Captain swings us around to avoid collision and we now try to depict that this is the usual procedure; there was nothing out of the ordinary happening. No need to worry, really we're just friendly Yukoners.

Perhaps we could have gotten away with this facade, but to my surprise, I notice off to our starboard side a dinghy that looks an awful lot like the one that is supposed to be attached to our stern. It is the damned dinghy! With the swing of the ship, the propeller cut the dinghy's lines. We have to go back into the maze of boats and rescue the dinghy.

There is no way that this can be construed as a usual procedure. I am laying on the bow, trying to "catch" the dinghy. We dodge boats and we try again. Then we try again; we should have charged admission. At this point, I want to strongly suggest that the Captain fish for the dinghy himself, but I am not yet a great helmsman. He is needed to steer the ship. I am being politically correct here. There are not many women out here in charge of vessels, come on girls.

Success! What is left of the line on the dinghy is hardly enough to secure her. You know what; I really don't care if we leave her to wander the harbours of the world forever at this point. Further back out into the harbour we skulk. We need room to breath, ponder our anchoring strategy and have at least 40 acres to turn this rig around in.

In another analogy, looking a gift horse in the mouth…in truth you really do need to check this out. There is a great big hole out here, in this very crowed harbour, lots of room. The question should have been, why?

To our portside is a 65 foot converted seiner. Very big, very solid, and as tough as a tugboat. Our anchor is set between the seiner and a sailboat registered out of "Utah". We have no room to talk here; we are, after all, registered out of Whitehorse.

Half an hour into the cocktail hour, the seiner has crept well into our 40 acres. The wind shifts; I can now spit and hit her transom. The captain of this seiner has let out enough rode to ride out any storm. In securing the safety of his ship, he has taken up a huge expanse of ocean. His ship has no keel and the wind dictates his direction. His swing path is 100 feet in all directions; he weighs 70 tonnes.

We are within 20 feet of his stern, if there are no storms in the night, we will be alright. If either of us drags any amount of anchor, we will end up on top of each other. Would you be able to sleep?

This has been another season of "sécurité" on the radio; gale-force winds have been tormenting much of the boating community. We have given up on the idea of exploring the Broughtons for this year. Johnstone Straight howls with fury and protest every time we try to chance it. Enough, already!

Winds, mostly nor'westers, have worn everyone out. In Newcastle Harbour, though, there is good protection from these demons. This Saturday morning, they announce that the wind will change direction and we face a sou'easter. The seas have room to build in this harbour, with a sou'easter.

With a malfunctioning windlass and a wildly swinging neighbour, we are setting ourselves up for disaster. We opt for the security of the harbour and tying up to the dock for safety. We need to recharge our systems. Audrey motors into Cameron Island, in Nanaimo, B.C.

Over the sputtering of Chayce's Harley noises, we hear shouting on the dock. The Captain and his son jump up.

"Holy crap… he's coming Straight for us." They run for the bow to try to ward off the ship.

I look through their legs on the bow and see a low-slung profile steaming towards us under full power. Military grey with that institutional look; I know that this is not a usual ship. The crew on the dock has missed catching his stern line, and with the wind howling and shoving against him, he has lost control.

The great grey bow is bearing down on top of us under full throttles, I yell at the Captain to get off of our bow. The captain of the Robert S attempts to lighten the impact. He rams the dock just in front of us with a mighty crash. Under the impact of this shock, a 50 foot yacht on the opposite side of the dock is sprung to the end of its lines. The lines snap back like a giant rubber band and retract the yacht hard against the dock. The dock appears to bend inward about 10 feet. The Robert S bounces back and slams into the dock again. This triple-hulled, ex-Navy Coast Guard cutter/gunboat is now headed at full speed towards the bow of the Audrey Eleanor…. (Continued in the next Adventure of the Audrey Eleanor, Robert S II)

P.S. I would like to thank Diane at motor vehicles for the gentle kick in the pants…this story is finally being published because Diane wanted to know where in the heck the adventures had gone. The Captain says if you don't do anything, then nothing will happen.

Sunshine Coast

THE ROBERT S II

In the last episode, the Robert S, an ex-Navy Coast Guard cutter/gunboat was on a high-speed collision course with the Audrey Eleanor.

The great grey bow of the Robert S is bearing down on the Audrey Eleanor. People are screaming, "Stop, stop!" A young man in his late twenties has been flung out of the back of this ex-military ship and is hanging precariously off the swim grid. The captain of the Robert S makes a last attempt to turn his ship from a collision course with the Audrey Eleanor; he battles the howling wind.

The Robert S swings hard to her portside, her beautiful wood tender with a heavy 25 horse Johnson kicker breaks loose from the davits that hold her to this ship's stern. Wildly swinging the heavy steel davits knock the power stanchion down to the dock. The young man on the swim grid has one arm and his head hanging just above the wate. The davits pass inches from his head. Impact! Our Captain has run down the gunnel, Audrey takes the hit hard to her bow.

Broken bow stem on the triple-planked hull of the Robert S after he charged the concrete pier at Cameron Island, Nanaimo, B.C.

BAM! The impact sends shudders through Audrey's hull and vibrates in her ribs. Ronnie and Chayce are still in in the saloon. I have jumped on the dock.

The Robert S is heading directly towards the concrete pier that forms the breakwater at Cameron Island. His bow slams into the concrete pier, and unbelievably, he has thrown the engines into reverse and is coming back on us amidships, again at full throttles. The Captain is screaming for someone to take control of the ship. The man on the swim grid yells that it is his great grandfather and he is 80 years old.

The Captain yells again, "Take the helm, take the helm, take the God-damned helm!"

On the dock, I'm shouting, "Get off the boat!"

Chayce's mother looks like she's in shock. I scream at her to give me the baby. She lifts her crying baby; I yank him out of her arms, out of the boat and run down the dock with him, he is screaming in terror.

The great grandson on the Robert S climbs up the transom and runs to take control. We are inches from a second collision. He slams the engines in forward. The props churn, the screaming of the engine, roar of the wind and churn of the wake slow down to a negative speed. In slow motion, we watch. Will it stop, or will it sink the Audrey Eleanor?

Our Captain begins to breathe again. The Robert S edges forward. He estimates that the Robert S stopped within six inches of our beam. Under that speed and with that power the impact would have put us on the bottom of this grey, wind-whipped sea.

We are afraid to look, but know that the damage done is above the water line. The dock in front of us has a cracked main beam and the stanchion is flopped over on the dock. Is anyone hurt? Chayce is crying, the poor baby doesn't know what is wrong. I hope he still loves his grandpa's boat after this scare; this ship is named after his great grandmother, whom he shares the same birthdate with. (Different year, you guys)

The Harbour Master is checking to make sure that no one is injured. People of all ages are pouring out of the Robert S. Everyone appears to be alright. It is a miracle that the great grandson survived after flopping around on the swim grid. We are in awe. There appears to be no damage. The Audrey Eleanor won the "Best Built Custom Vessel" at the wooden boat show in Pender Harbour last year, but it is unbelievable that she could survive this without harm.

We go to meet the Captain and first mate of the Robert S. Bob and Marva are clearly in shock. This is their home. Bob worked on the Robert

S when it was stationed out of Juneau, Alaska, during the WWII. His ship was a gunboat in the "unknown" war that was waged with Japan in Alaska. During WWII, there were two 30 calibre and one 50 calibre machine guns mounted on its decks. When the Robert S was de-commissioned, Bob bought the ship and converted it into a home for himself and his family. The Robert S is named after Bob's father. Bob is 80 years old. This trip north to Canada and Princess Louisa Inlet were designated to be his last on the command bridge.

It appears that they have insurance. At this point, we aren't too concerned; Audrey seems fine. Marva passes over personal information and insurance details. They have plans to leave in the morning. On board are their children, grandchildren and great-grandchildren. This is a family outing designed to celebrate the reign of their captain.

Marva and Bob decide to come over to the Audrey Eleanor as some documents are originals and they don't want to part with them. I copy down the information, and off in the corner the captains compare notes. When it is time to leave, Bob gets lost. He is disorientated and doesn't know where he is. We are hoping that this is a temporary condition due to the shock of the crash; his great grandson came close to losing his life.

Marva states that they will be in touch. What I suspect is that they have never dealt with an insurance claim before. After they leave, I notice that the insurance policy is for a 1999 Chrysler.

Curiouser and curiouser…the wharfinger, Warren, does a follow-up on the dock. I ask him if he has ever dealt with a U.S. insurance claim. The marina will possibly be looking for damages as well; he hasn't. We decide that we need to determine if they actually have marine insurance.

What to do? Call the RCMP, of course, that's what you do when you crash the car or the car crashes you.

The RCMP sends me to the Coast Guard. The Coast Guard sends me back to the RCMP. Motor vehicle, motor vessel… no one knows what to do. I talk to a recently-transferred RCMP lady from Whitehorse; she is most helpful and sends a young officer down to deal with the "boat people". They have never done this before; we offer excellent training. How on earth can anyone take a claim seriously if it hasn't been reported to some type of authority? The crew on the Robert S don't take kindly to the Queen's cowboys showing up on their deck.

Maybe this why they run around suing each other down there; they don't have to report anything, apparently. We tell Bob and Marva that in Canada we have to file a legitimate report in order to further any type of insurance claim. Tempers deflate. Bob and Marva disappear into the hold, never to be seen again. Warren, the wharfinger, suggests that we take a closer look at Audrey; he has discovered more damage to his docks.

The Robert S has cracked his bow stem and popped planks on his bow, his hull is triple-planked. The transom is sporting a hole about a foot in diameter. Our Captain walks down the dock and looks back. The planks on Audrey's bow on the starboard side have been popped and her seams are split on both sides. It is difficult to see the popped planks from the dock. The general discussion is whether we have cracked our ribs and bow stem as well. We will have to be hauled out for inspection.

If her main structure is damaged, will this be the end of the Audrey Eleanor? And does the Robert S have insurance to cover his liability? This crew will be held in bondage at Stones Marina to cover costs if they don't…. catch the next Adventure of the Audrey Eleanor, The Robert S III.

P.S. I would like to wish my brother Joel a Happy Birthday (little late, sorry). I wish for you happiness and good health, this is the year to do it.

Sunshine Coast

THE ROBERT S III: JOY

After a collision with the Robert S, the Audrey Eleanor is under repair on the hard in Stones Marina, Nanaimo, B.C.

In the previous episodes, the Audrey Eleanor had come under attack by an ex-Navy cutter/gunboat. The crew now need to determine if Audrey has met the end of her days. The other consideration is whether the US boat that hit her has insurance to cover the damage that he has done.

Sunday roars in with gale-force winds. The Robert S remains dockside; their plans to motor to Princess Louisa Inlet have been altered due to the thrashings of the Furies. There is tension on the dock. I'm sure the captain of the Robert S is feeling terrible about the damage he's done. They are likely not in the celebratory mood that this final trip was supposed to create. There is little movement from our neighbours across the watery alleyway.

As the possibility of losing our grand lady sinks in, we aren't feeling real neighbourly either. It will be a double jeopardy if our damages and costs aren't covered. The All State Farm Insurance Co. of the U.S.A. doesn't give out information on the weekend; we have to wait until Monday to find out if the Robert S has marine insurance. The reality is that the Robert S could have motored away to sea by then. We aren't taking on water, which is good, but the lack of knowing is weighing heavy on us. The loss builds in our minds.

Monday morning begins with the harbour authority showing up to assess damages to their docks. A main beam is cracked and the stanchion has to be resecured. A thick rubber bumper built of 4 inches of solid rubber has been cracked on the concrete pier and the water and sewer lines have been split. What an amazing ship, it's hard to believe that the Robert S is still afloat. A plastic or fibreglass boat would have crumpled. Mind you, the damage to us and the docks would have been less as well.

Remember the big seiner out in the harbour with the huge swing radius? He was one of the reasons that we came dockside, to avoid getting caught up in his rode (anchor line). There looks to be a pile up of some type just out of eye sight, Through the b'nocs, I can make out the mess. It's a rat's nest of boats; the harbour patrol is headed out to try to untangle the snare. Snuggled up close and tight to the seiner is not one, but two fair-sized sailboats, 35 and 25 feet, respectively. This whole party is bumping and grinding into a landing craft and they are all heading towards the rocky shore…remember to trust your gut, people.

Whether it was a better choice to come to shore to avoid him, I suppose we will never know. I lose sight of them and wonder at their misfortune and damage.

Dave Mallioux, harbour supervisor, shows up dockside and things happen. The weekend wharfinger, Warren, (say that five times fast) has filed an in-depth report and Dave is here to follow up. They have determined that the Robert S has insurance and have a claim number for us. Hallelujah, the Goddess has returned and there is sunlight in our lives again. Winds whipping up waves (I'm into this "W" thing) won't allow us to leave port. The extra moorage is a concern and I feel that I am watching our savings fly off across the ocean. Dave senses our concern and tells us not to worry, the Port of Nanaimo has offered us moorage until the damage gets sorted out. This includes the return to the dock to regroup once the work is done. We can reserve a spot.

Last year I had a breast cancer scare here, and now this. I want to go home to return to Nanaimo no more and never again! Dave's thoughtful consideration took away the bite, thank you Dave. The staff at the harbour authority were fabulous, they put up with the paperwork shuffle needed by the insurance company. You know what I mean. By the way, Tara from the Discovery Marina in Campbell River, you have NO idea how much I appreciate you bringing down the Captain's hearing aids!

We are in the sling heading for the "hard". I hate this part; our lady's bare bottom is exposed and swinging high above our heads. The slings have to be positioned just so, so that she isn't crushed inward by her own weight. She is at Stones and we will finally know how much she has been hurt.

Tony Koch is the marine surveyor. He tap tap taps with his custom hammer.

"Hmm," he says. "Hmmm."

What in the hell is hmmm? We will have to find a shipwright that is qualified to remove more of her planking; with what access we have, Tony can't determine how much damage has been done. How about an ultrasound?

Do you have any idea how hard it is to find someone who is qualified to do this work? The old trades have become a vanishing act. There are plenty of suggestions, but the reality is that the craftspeople are fading out of this time. We stumble on the Noyce brothers. The Captain had actually called them prior to the accident with questions about a windlass problem and had talked to Dave. Dave had given him a simple remedy that worked… our kind of guys. Paul shows up to do the internal. More hmm, hmms.

Paul has a limited amount of time, this appears to be a longer than usual project, and he has a prior commitment. Regardless, what is the diagnosis? Well, the planks have been popped and a few seams split, but nothing internal. This is an amazing ship, he states, I've never seen one built like this, she's a tough lady.

You can't imagine the relief. We don't want Audrey to end her days in our care. She has years to go yet and will out-live us with the right owners. THIS IS A GREAT DAY!

Paul can fit a few hours in here and there. Dave, who is his partner and brother, has a broken right hand; of course, he is right handed. The bonus is that I am now in wooden boat building 101. I get to caulk and plug, I like it. The Captain is trying to find Honduras mahogany planks that are a true 1inch x 6 inch x 12 feet long. It's an endangered species; we live in a floating wood museum, apparently. Nothing is simple. It really doesn't matter, it's like the thought of cancer...once the scare is gone, anything is possible and nothing is really that important anyway.

So here we sit, 20 feet in the air. The view is incredible. People rush to catch the ferry, seagulls curse each other, I can feel my skin sucking up the salt brine that is carried on a light breeze. It's a sight to see Silvia and Bill haul their boxer dog, Zar, 20 feet up in a sling for bedtime onboard the Salubrious, a magnificent wooden sailboat from Orcas Island.

Wooden boats don't do well out of the salt water, being out of the water could cause Audrey to dry out and crack. These accommodations are hard on us; there is no inside potty. I have to climb 20 feet down the ladder to get to the flush toilet and showers. Last Valentine's Day, the Captain installed a flush toilet for me at Wolf Creek. We had lived in construction through the winter. Presents like that you never forget... chocolates come and chocolates go. I was glad that we had a mild winter last year.

We still don't know if All State Farm Insurance are the "friends" they claim to be, they are taking their corporate time. Audrey has to be fixed, she's part of our family and that is just what you do regardless.

P.S. We have been on a waitlist for moorage at Madeira Park Marina for five years. Ian, the Harbour Master, called a few days ago. He was having a hard time managing to fit us in, but he said, "Dawn, you and the Captain just bring her home and we'll figure it out." I'm still pretty misty about that one; of course, there will be another Adventure of the Audrey Eleanor. (There is heaven on earth; it might be the Sunshine Coast.)

Sunshine Coast

SALTSPRING ISLAND

Simply saying the name Saltspring Island causes gentle breezes to whisper through my mind and fluffy sheep to jump unbidden over my snob hurdles. Directly behind the sheep are groups of people stating that we "simply must visit the Island." I am a snob.

Attending anything that represents the "thing to do" automatically causes a shut down in my systems and drives me in the opposite direction. Never having been much of a groupie or follower, period, I am sure that I have missed some life-altering fads that drive the marketplace. The real word, of course, is the dollar place. This mantra may have caused me to miss some very important teachings; although I doubt it. Missing a visit to Saltspring Island however, would have been a loss. I am glad that we reconsidered.

Julia sings the Stones' song Painted Black on Saltspring Island

Audrey slices through the oily grey ocean this misty morning. Biting gusts of wind tormented us last night and forced a sleep over at Maple Bay. The grey sea is smooth this dawn. There is no distinction between the ocean and the sky. The Swartz Bay ferry floats on the horizon. The swell and brake of wake behind the ferry draws a dividing line that leads towards the heavens. I am at the helm and need to get our nose through these giant swells that the ferry leaves behind. The bow rises and falls with the swell; we swish through the water, gently riding the wake. Initially, ferry wakes scared the daylights out of me; I am acquiring experience.

Ganges Harbour on Saltspring is our destination this day. This is Friday morning; we have arranged to be here for the famous farmer's market on Saturday. Our cruise from Maple Bay is a short one, and we arrive well before noon.

During the busy season, this harbour is solid with anchored boats. As it is, we have several spaces to consider dropping the hook. Large, bright yellow and floating just to our starboard side is a mooring buoy. We have not tied to a buoy in a harbour before. I call the harbour master and ask whom it belongs to and what the protocol is.

It is not the property of the harbour authority of Saltspring. A private buoy is supposed to have the owner's name and phone number on it so that you are able to call and ask if you can use it. This one has no ID. We can tie to it, and expect at some point to have to either leave or give the owners money. This harbour is beginning to fill up; we are surprised as this is October, the quiet season. Paying for the mooring buoy is fine, if we are asked to leave, however, there might be no space left to anchor later in the day. What on earth is going on in this place? Boats are charging in towards the docks. Have we missed a bad weather forecast?

SS Marina is at the head of the bay. I radio in to see if they are accepting transient boats. They are and my goodness, today is the start of winter rates. Instead of paying a dollar a foot plus hydro, we pay fifty cents plus hydro…it's a steal. We will go dockside. I have my bow and amidships lines coiled and ready to tie off; we mostly dock by ourselves. Today, we have a reception line. There are four people waiting to catch our ropes, how nice and so much less stress for me!

One gentleman is CLEARLY in command. I get the impression that he may be instructing two of the others in the art of sailing. The fourth person is the harbour mistress, Leslie. In a challenging voice, the commander asks if I "possibly" have my midships line ready. Of course I do, I say, we usually do this by ourselves. The harbour mistress begins to choke a little and has to cover her face with her sleeve. The truth is that it is only in the last year that I have realized the sense of the midship line and begun to use it more in place of the bowline. The commander says no more, I thank him very much for his assistance and I mean this.

Green leaves, flowers st their fullest bloom...there is brilliant colour and smells of fresh cut grass and mouldering apples...this is October. It's still summer here. Where to start, there is so much to see. As it happens. we have arrived for the wooden working boat show at Ganges. This is the reason for the charge of boats in the harbour. Beautiful wooden fish boats converted to live a boards, and boats that are still working the seas. How lucky is this, we run into friends that we have met at other wooden boat shows. There is a relaxed atmosphere with this beer-drinking crowd. It is difficult to tear ourselves away from these down to earth folk.

We should explore the village. Love at first sight, we discover a restaurant that is constructed around a large tree. The menu looks wonderful, and tonight they will feature local talent singing their own versions of the "Stones". We are starved for relaxation and entertainment, having spent a month under repair and living in yet another construction zone while Audrey was being fixed. Do you remember anticipating a dance when you were in high school? I am feeling this. The waitress suggests that we do not arrive any later than six in order to get a seat. This is exciting.

By the time we return, the only seats left leave us snuggling up close to the tree's trunk that grows through the roof of this funky little restaurant. Patrons are provided with blankets to cover knees and cold bottoms. Stars twinkle through the leaves of the overhead canopy that the tree provides. The salmon melts in our mouths, and the wine is one of our favourite New Zealand varieties, chilled perfectly. I am wiggling in my seat waiting for the show to begin.

Artists and instruments are collecting in any spare spot in the restaurant and flowing over and out onto the tables and chairs set outside on the patio. Sleepy children are cuddled in corners, the older ones send off waves of anticipation, either of their parents may be performing and who knows if they won't get called up to do some back up with a tambourine.

This reminds me of the old Frostbite Festivals when they were held in what is now the transportation museum in Whitehorse. The loss of that era still bites me.

We bet on whether one of the musicians is wearing a wig or if one human could possibly grow that enormous black curly head of hair. He steps up to the mike and as he announces that the show will begin. He bows low and doffs his hair. I lose.

There are over 20 different musicians here to pay tribute to the Rolling Stones. Julia is the first up and she does a low-key version of Painted Black. As I listen to her shyly croon to the mike, I realize that this is possibly a song that her grandmother danced to. I hate when these realizations hit me in the gut like that. God…

Brown Sugar sets the boots to stomping and the crowd howls out the chorus at the top of their lungs. Song after song is re-visited and revised. The audience dances in their seats and the musicians are warmed up and collaborating with each other. Energy is whizzing through space and charging up the singers, the crowd from the musicians are no longer discernable, this is music meshing…

Kids are up doing back up singing and tambourine shaking, no one wants this to end. I refuse to believe that all good things must come to an end. What negative person started that? This memory will stay with us, and I'm sure everyone else too, for many years to come. Do they experience this every weekend? What a place! Tomorrow is the market and the boat show. I am looking forward to seeing what this island has to offer in the way of garden veggies, food products and arts. This is the Garden of Eden in Canada, after all.

P.S. Have any of you heard of The Red Bastard? If you are interested, Google him. His performance is startling to say the least. We saw him at the arts centre on Saltspring…I am at a loss for words with regards to him. He is world-renowned in his field. His performance floods or ebbs depending on audience participation. Possibly, this performance was extreme due to the number of people that were intent on participating in this show. I am still left questioning a sense of depth at his intent or whether it was simply narcissistic.

Sunshine Coast

RAINBOW SONG ON SALTSPRING

Sailboat repair in Ganges Harbour, on Saltspring Island.

Saturday morning arrives muffled in grey. Not exactly fog, just silent with still water and pearly-silver skies. It is surreal, seeing sailboats float in the glimmering clouds…no, I have not been smoking anything.

Our next door neighbour is a sailboat with a man attached to its mast. The man is 25 feet in the air. He is attempting to do one-handed repair work. The Captain is very happy that he does not have to do this type of aerial maintenance.

Saturday markets on Saltspring Island are legendary. Who knew that there were purple carrots? We have been paying attention to the genetic altering of foods and what we eat. They should be required to post if alterations are made to the food in the grocery store. (Basically they breed out the good stuff in food to make it look pretty so that we will eat it or alter it so that it will last forever.)

There is emphasis on heritage seeds and organic farming here. Some species of carrot are purple. This was not as appealing to the eye, apparently, and so they are now that beautiful orange colour. What nutrients were lost in the process? Goat cheese arrives, topped with flower petals, flavours of lemon and truffle, with a dash of garlic. It is really much better fresh, I have to say. The Captain is fond of goats milk in any form; I need some convincing.

Artisan breads fill baskets; peppers are mounded in hills of bright oranges, reds, greens and purples. Baskets of shiny blackberries sit beside freshly-baked pies of the same flavour. Apples, apples everywhere and yes, they are offered as drink…soft or hard cider. There is only so much room on the boat, and we have outdone ourselves with the varieties of goat cheese we have purchased. How much can the Captain eat? We buy a rope rug; this is a tying art, you know. (Just had to do that)

A puckish young man approaches us; he is carrying a didgeridoo, a small bow and arrow type object and has a really nice smile. He introduces himself as Paly Rainbow Song…we are on Saltspring Island people. He really is a nice man, I like his striped, billowy pants. He says he would like to try his invention on us, but only if we don't suffer from epileptic seizures. It has to do with light flickering from the sun's rays and his little bow like apparatus. I have heard that flickering lights will set off seizures of different types. We agree to aid in the experiment and guarantee that we haven't had a seizure yet today. (I'm on a roll)

Somehow, I miss the total intent of this experiment. The Captain takes the lead, Paly places the didgeridoo on his shoulder, tells him to shut his eyes and look directly at the sun. With his face directed towards the sun the Captain shuts his eyes, Paly spins the bow type object in front of the Captains eyes as he begins a heartbeat style vibration on the didgeridoo. I can see that the Captain is smiling, all looks well.

My turn. I love the didgeridoo, what I am looking for behind closed eyes, I am not sure of. I see black and white electric-type flashes with four small white boxes. I can open my eyes now; Paly looks at me expectantly. I smile and thank him with a donation towards future research. I am simply happy to have had the mini didgeridoo concert. We continue on; this is not yet done with.

Blasts from steam whistles fill the harbour as the Working Wooden Boat Show winds down. The "Breeze", a beautiful old tugboat, appears to be signalling for a motor by. All participating boats still in harbour now start their engines, with horns honking and whistles thrilling. A procession begins to leave the harbour with the Breeze in the lead.

The twin Otters are trying to maintain a flight schedule in the middle of this confusion. Planes are taxiing out of the harbour alongside the boats. It appears that the planes are taking off within inches of boat masts; they skim over the tops of the buoys, which bob in their wake. Smoke from the tugs fills the air; the sound and motion is chaotic commotion. I am sad to leave this Garden of Eden. It is a special place to visit.

The Captain has an incredible ability to sniff out Yukon connections. While on our way to Saltspring Island, I mentioned that we had been forced to spend a night at Maple Bay Marina on Vancouver Island. Maple Bay has a weighs!

We have had to haul Audrey out in the past with a sling. While this method has worked, it is not the best way to handle a 30 tonne wooden boat. A weighs presents the option of placing your boat on a rail type system, then the whole weighs is pulled ashore with the boat sitting on top. There is no pressure as in the lift; it is much easier on everyone. Weighs of this type are becoming more difficult to find. In the south. we have found a weighs on Quadra Island at Cape Mudge, and now this one in Maple Bay.

This is a form of insanity. We have just spent a month on the hard in a shipyard, and we are snooping around yet another yard. The Captain is headed towards a large, covered wooden boat set up on blocks close to the bank. It is easy to see that she has beautiful lines even with the partial covering of the tarp. Almost hidden under the tarp are two salty type guys that look like they know what they are doing. It is apparent that they need a break; as soon as the Captain closes in on them they pause in their work.

The ship is the "Grail Dancer", a traditional schooner crafted after the hull lines of the "Emma C Berry", which was a Noank Well Smach from 1866. LOA is 61 feet with a beam of 15 feet.

Construction of this beautiful schooner began in 1986 on Thetis Island, B.C. It was launched in 2000. The rigging and systems took another five years and, as is normal, the work continues. Some wooden boat enthusiasts compare wood boats to plastic boats as real flowers to plastic flowers, a little more work, perhaps, but how can you compare one to the other?

I am listening to this mingling of minds and something about the one gentleman is vaguely familiar. As usual, once the length and style of each others' boat has been discussed, a myriad of techniques and styles are sifted through, and once the "hmms" have settled, the Yukon gets mentioned. Oh yes, this sets off yet another discussion. The gentleman repairing his own ship, the Grail Dancer, is none other than Wayne Loiselle, shipwright extraordinaire.

Yukoners can thank him for the restoration work on the SS Klondike and the SS Keno. He spent several years working on both projects. The restorations, in turn, helped him to finance the construction of the Grail Dancer.

Positive things work in circles and I am always amazed at how far the ripples of the Yukon extend into areas that you least expect. When we had first purchased the Audrey Eleanor, we had searched for Wayne, wanting his advice on anything that pertained to wooden boats.

Wayne asked us to say hello to Vince, the round town photographer at the "Star".

P.S. Back to Paly Rainbow Song…Moby's is the pub at the top of our dock on Saltspring Island. We stopped in for a beer our last night in town. Our barmaid asked about our visit and we mentioned Paly. She asked what colours we saw while he twirled his magic bow. I had suffered terribly with a migraine headache for a week, life in the shipyard was hard on me. I have developed a chemical intolerance and was concerned about the headache. Paly did his rainbow song on me, my headache left and did not return. I don't know if it was a coincidence. The strange thing is that I did not see rainbow colours and had no idea that I was supposed to. I saw black and white. She said that this was the first she had heard of the lack of colour in the light flickers, everyone sees colours…and that is the rest of the story.

Sunshine Coast

THE CONCLUSION

My incredible son, Bob, dreams of sailing to distant horizons while at the helm of the Audrey Eleanor.

We left Audrey in Campbell River for a month while we went to a family reunion in Lethbridge, Alberta, and then headed south to Walla Walla, Washington State, to visit with THE Audrey Eleanor Cousins who our ship is named after. She turned 85 this year. We returned to Canada and attempted to resume our summer holiday. Two days after we cast off lines in Campbell River. the Robert S, a 1942 ex-gunboat, hit us at Cameron Island in Nanaimo.

There weren't a lot of pleasurable times onboard this year, between the rats and repairs. People keep life interesting though; they are the actual joy between the agonies. They are what made this summer worthwhile.

Continuously, the Captain has Yukon encounters. Like minds are attracted to like geography I'm sure. We seem to run into ex-Yukoners within a close proximity to the water, or at least the ones that we have a common interest with and there are lots of them. We are strolling on the Nanaimo waterfront one beautiful afternoon, looking for ice cream.

A trio passes us, heading in the opposite direction; one of the men is wearing a hat that is similar to the Captain's. The comment, "nice hat", simultaneously from both men sets off an hour-long conversation about the Yukon.

The lady in the group is Jeanie Smith, born in Whitehorse. She left by the age of twelve. Her partner is Alfred, and he lives on an island. Alfred was once featured in the Whitehorse Star as the first person, I believe, who purchased a "round the world" ticket on Pan American Airlines. He has invited us to visit him on his island and drop our anchor in the bay close to his home.

Alfred makes plum wine and has offered to show me how. I'm hooked on the invitation to visit him on an island; the making of plum wine is taking this opportunity way over the top. Jeanie is my kind of lady, I am really excited about this friendship. I miss the robustness and colour of the old Yukoners. They may all be on that island. I know they are hiding somewhere from regulation; I want to go there.

Knock, knock. A solid rap on Audrey's hull announces visitors. A lofty set of persons who have just arrived back in Nanaimo. They have seen the For Sale sign on Audrey and are curious.

The "Three Cheers" accumulated over 300 hours of engine time on a sailboat excursion to Alaska and back. That translates into LOTS of sea time. Nanaimo is their homeport, but they don't want the trip to end, so are spending the night 400 yards away from their home berth. We understand.

I am in the galley, finishing up an amazing black cod chowder when they arrive. While I set the chowder out for our guests, the question of destinations arises. I say that before the summer is through I want to go and visit Alfred and Jeanie on Alfred's island.

"Oh," states our lady visitor. "Yes, I know that island. Tom Rosco's brother lives there as well." Tom Rosco is a friend of ours in Whitehorse.

I ask this woman who she is and where she is from and she smiles and says, "I am Terrylynn Gold and my partner's name is Siggy. I am from Whitehorse."

This is jaw dropping. It's a small world after all; it's a small, small world. Yes, we still offer food to people before we know their names; it is an old northern tradition. This is another couple that we have been so very fortunate to meet.

P.K and Julia are the crew on board the "Havfruen", a 100 foot sailboat built in New Zealand. This over 60, possibly closer to 70 year old couple are the ONLY crew. We think they are missing marbles. They have just returned from a two year trip to Mexico via the west coast of California, Oregon and Washington, in October.

We have yet to talk to anyone who has had a pleasant journey using this return route, and especially at this time of year. You are bucking currents and huge waves the entire way. I believe this could be way worse than coming down from Alaska to Vancouver Island in October and November.

P.K said that at a point of exhaustion, he left the helm to Julia. He desperately needed sleep. Lying on the couch in the saloon, he could hear a huge booming sound as their ship landed on the waves. This was followed by the sshhing sound of air rushing past the gunnels. At that point P.K. realized that this sound was 90 metric tonnes of ship "catching air." Unbelievable!

Yes, there is a for sale sign on the Audrey Eleanor. We have not listed her on any website or with a broker. In the Captain's words, she is for sale depending on who wants to buy her. As part of the insurance process, we had Audrey surveyed twice, once for damages and then once again when the work was done.

She still has a wicked body and her heart is pure gold. Finding her the moorage of our dreams has taken the edge off of selling her; we know now that she is being cared for. It becomes easy to dream of venturing out on to the "high" seas again.

The sale price on her is $59,000, well below the appraised value. She will be sold to someone who will continue the love affair and have the ability to work on her (or at least want to learn like we still are). We realize that enthusiasm doesn't always translate into cash; this is the person that we have priced the boat for. In the meantime, we have next summer's cruise planned out.

While we were sitting on the hard at Stones, we were approached by a very excited gentleman. He had always wanted to see a hull design of our type. This design had, in truth, caused great bafflement to the Captain. Audrey is built like a giant speedboat and had hit speeds of 22 knots (with Chrysler built gas guzzlers). We think we are flying at 10 knots with our twin Perkins diesels these days.

This gentleman is Ted Aussom, proud owner of the "Privateer" and secretary for the Canadian Fleet of the International Classic Yacht Association. CYA is dedicated to the promotion, preservation, restoration and maintenance of fine, old, power-driven pleasure craft... a mouthful. He is very excited about the Audrey Eleanor and asks us if we would be interested in joining their association.

We have avoided clubs and associations like they are members of the rat family; Ted assures us that they drink beer and cuss. It is not that we don't mind wine in crystal on occasion; regulations are suffocation in my mind and both of us do prefer life on the edge. When you possess a rare wooden yacht, you can duck in and out of "society" as you wish and be welcome. We prefer this freedom and lack of expectation.

He is a really, really nice guy and the effect of that is we are now members of the CYA. In the New Year, you will be able to see pictures of the Audrey Eleanor on their website, www.classicyacht.org. This particular society has already offered invaluable information on all aspects of classic power yachting. The Commodore, Mike O'Brien, is very personable and we look forward to getting to know these people more in the coming years.

P.S. We have had fun sharing these true stories with all of you. The Captain says if it isn't fun DON'T DO IT! Health and happiness always...watch for the book. Terry, I promise it is still coming. Thanks so much for all of your comments and enthusiasm. xxx ooo

Sunshine Coast

OUR FRIEND, RICHARD BOYCE

An Audrey Eleanor Adventure for Richard Boyce

Richard hanging over the transom, conversing with Captain Rick as Rick clears his propellers in Hoonah, Alaska, circa 2007.

"That's quite the boat." I look out of the doorway and squint into the sun. A "rojo" Australian shepherd is attached to the jean-clad leg standing on the dock. I can't quite make out his face, but catch sight of a grey beard with remnants of rust and the outline of a ball cap in the glare. He steps sideways. "Better?" he asks. "Yeah, thanks," I reply.

Eyes that have stared and strained to catch horizons in dusk and dark are deeply crinkled with laugh lines.

"How did you come by the name Audrey Eleanor?" he asks.

"I named her after Rick's mom," I state.

"My Boat is the Eleanor S, named her after my oldest daughter, Ellie."

"Not too many boats with the name Eleanor attached to 'em."

An easy connection is formed. I am introduced to his leg attachment, Rosie, the red Aussie shepherd.

Richard has three red-haired daughters. Ellie, Lucinda (Lucy) and Karen, his baby. I never got to meet Ellie; she was off chasing glaciers. I believe she got caught on an Alaskan glacier in a marriage ceremony, though she headed towards New Zealand after the wedding. Both her and her husband being enthralled with the anomalies of Mother Earth and all. Would have loved to have met her, Richard's voice would shine with pride and wonderment at the life she was leading.

And then we have Lucinda; Lucinda was working on the Fjordland, which runs a passenger service between Haines, Skagway and Juneau during the summer months. Richard's home is located outside of Haines, Alaska, up a mostly goat trail of a road that carries you up and up and up. Difficult to get to even if you are a goat.

Driving into Haines, Alaska, you may have noticed a sign before you get to town that states, "Free Camping and Seniors Discount". This is Richard's back yard, complete with sense of welcome and humour. It was much easier for Lucinda to stay onboard the Eleanor S in between shifts on the Fjordland.

Lean frame leaning against the gunnel, he pokes his head through the doorway of the Audrey Eleanor.

"Do you happen to notice my boat at night?"

"For sure, Richard, Lucinda is pretty quiet. What's up?"

"Well, I am kinda worried about who's keeping her company."

"You want me to spy on Lucy?"

"It's not really spying. I am her dad, I worry."

He talked about a time when he and a few other fathers in Haines had seriously considered rounding up their daughters and sequestering them to life on Eldred Rock (a miserable piece of rock located south in the Lynn Canal)...or at least until they reached an age of sanity. Whether he was talking about the daughters or the fathers, I am not sure. Lucy has a temper to match her gorgeous red hair. She arrives in a fury.

"My father says that he has spies onboard the Audrey Eleanor! How dare you spy on me!"

I am out of arms reach I can laugh.

"Not a chance, girl. He asked, I suggested he talk to you."

Well, his response was to tell Lucy that we were spying regardless.

"That cagey old man, I know his game."

We all ponder revenge.

Karen is the horse child, loves horses, breathes horses and leaves home to attend university, where she can pursue the "equine love".

I was fortunate to have her and her dad spend the night with us in Whitehorse; she had to have dental work done. Her father and I pored over marine charts while she watched television, an unusual opportunity for this daughter of an Alaskan fisherman. An easy, pleasant evening of nothing special with special people; sometimes that's all that's needed to create a memory.

My son, Bob, and daughter-in-law, Shellane, my baby girl Kait and I take the "Nice Aft" over to Haines on Saturday, May 10 2013. I am being treated to a special Mother's Day. I sip Mimosas, cuddled up warm beside my son. We have motored over and are hoping to sail back. I am excited to be returning to Haines!

We tie up at the end of the dock and I am looking forward to seeing old friends, Richard in particular. I have my cards with me, the *www. thewhitegirl.ca* cards with the bright beadwork on the front; I am hoping to share this latest venture with old friends. They have their names in some of the Adventures of the Audrey Eleanor, stories and I think they might not mind?

The Eleanor S is moored in her home berth; it feels funny not to see the Audrey Eleanor tied across from her. Her hull shines white and the big fluorescent floats are bunched on her side like happy birthday balloons. There are coffee cups on the table inside of the Eleanor S; good, Richard must be in town. He has been spending winters south, working on a sailboat, admitting that the dark of winter has been getting to him. I had emailed him over the winter, no response but often there is no email where boats go.

I take a few cards and tuck them in his window, where he will see them. As I go down the docks, I tuck a few more in boats that I know. We decide to go to the Fogcutter and see who's in town and what's going on.

It is pretty quiet; I don't notice that old reprobate, Ron Martin, in the corner, but the barmaid mentions that he is in fact over talking with his daughter. Ron and I once exchanged fresh fish for smoked fish. For 60 Sockeye, I would smoke 30 for him and keep the rest; it was a great deal for both of us.

Ron, or should I say, Mr. Martin, comes over and I introduce him to my family. He fills me in on the fishery, the fact that Stan is doing well, Carl and Jenny are back. I mention Richard's name and a strange look comes over his face. In a soft voice he says, "Girl, you know that Richard drowned last summer?"

My head spins and I feel faint. I stare at Ron in disbelief, he can see that I am not understanding,

"He fell overboard last July, Karen was onboard with him. He surfaced twice and then went down, they never found him."

Blood rushes to my head, tears fall unbidden down my face.

"No, he was one of the good guys, I never got to say goodbye…Oh my god, Rick will take this so hard!"

We had been in Haines on May 24th last year and had missed Richard by seconds at every coffee shop in Haines. An hour for coffee would turn into half a day, as we repaired the world and Rick and Richard discussed possible welding solutions for Richard's generation problems up on the mountain. There would always be tomorrow to catch up. Tomorrow will never come.

In heavy rain gear and boots, he did not stand a chance; he had no floatation devices on. His daughter, Karen, threw him a life ring, but the tides had been high and currents ran strong. Rain gear by itself is cumbersome and bulky when you are hauling fish and nets; adding floatation devices can be a danger in itself. There are now suspenders that are floatation devices and a fund has been set up in Haines known as the ***Richard Boyce Inflatable Suspender Memorial Fund.***

Who can even imagine what young Karen was feeling? A friend from another boat took the long, long ride with her back to Haines. It is a 45 mile trip. Apparently, she pulled the Eleanor S into her home berth, tied her up like she had been taught to by her dad, and then collapsed into her older sister's arms.

In August, 2007, in Hoonah, Alaska, we were so happy to see the Eleanor S round the corner with Lucinda and Richard on board. Richard was worried that he had something caught in his prop at that time. Rick put on his dive suit and checked and cleaned the screw for him.

In the morning we pulled out of Hoonah, heading south with the Audrey Eleanor. As I went aft to remove the line, I noticed a gigantic barnacle shell on the gunnel, a good-bye present from Lucinda. I have it still.

That winter, we were in La Paz Mexico. I happened to have a "live" connection with Richard on the internet; asked him where Lucy was, his reply was, "No place were anyone would know how to find her."

"And where is that?"

"La Paz, Mexico, onboard the Sea Lion, a National Geographic ship. She is third mate."

We had just stopped to watch the Sea Lion dock and had noticed a crew member on the top deck with brilliant red hair. Did not think for a second it was Lucy and it was.

He surely loved his girls. Our good friend Richard Boyce, one of the very great guys who leaves a space that no one can fill, missing at sea by Mab Island, Alaska, July 4, 2012, aged 63.

Made in the USA
Charleston, SC
18 November 2016